MASSACHUSETTS
Recipes For All Seasons

Text by
Ruth and Milton Bass
Lynda Morgenroth
Anne Morris

LEISURE
TIME
PUBLISHING
INC.
DALLAS,TX

Published by the Massachusetts Department of Food and Agriculture, Boston, Massachusetts, in association with Leisure Time Publishing, a division of Heritage Worldwide, Incorporated, Dallas, Texas.

Publisher	Rodney L. Dockery
General Manager & Editorial Director	Caleb Pirtle III
Executive Editor	Ken Lively
Managing Editor	Sheri Harris
Regional Publishing Director	Pam Porter
Project Editor	Betty Miser
Food Editor	Diane Luther
Editorial Assistants	Susan Lee, Sarah Vasil
Art Director	Lynn Herndon Sullivan
Production Coordinator	Erin Gregg
Production Manager	Vickie Craig

Special thanks to Commissioner August Schumacher Jr., Janet Christensen, Chief, Bureau of Markets, and the entire Massachusetts Department of Food and Agriculture staff.

Photography provided by the Massachusetts Office of Travel and Tourism, Diane J. Baedecker and the Massachusetts Department of Food and Agriculture, and compliments of Robert S. Arnold and Old Sturbridge Village.

Cover Photograph: Harvesting pumpkins on Freeman Farm, Old Sturbridge Village. Photo by Robert S. Arnold.

First Printing

Manufactured in the United States of America

Printed by:
Heritage Worldwide, Inc.
9029 Directors Row
Dallas, Texas 75247
Telephone: (214) 630-4300

CONTENTS

Acknowledgments IV

Foreword V

The North Shore 1

Appetizers & Snacks 19

Beverages 27

Greater Boston 31

Breads 51

Cape Cod 59

Soups 75

Salads 83

Worcester 93

Sauces 99

Main Dishes 103

The Islands 111

Meats & Fish 123

Plymouth 133

Pasta 139

Pioneer Valley 147

Vegetables 159

The Berkshires 169

Desserts 183

Cakes 191

Pies 199

Cookies 207

Buyer's Guide 211

Index 215

ACKNOWLEDGEMENTS

The Massachusetts Department of Food and Agriculture would like to extend a special thanks to the following, whose participation has been so vital to the success of this cookbook:

Cape Cod Cranberry Growers Association
Massachusetts Agriculture in the Classroom
Massachusetts Association of Roadside Stands
Massachusetts Aquaculture Association
Massachusetts Christmas Tree Association
Massachusetts Cultivated Blueberry Association
Massachusetts Farmstead Cheese Association
Massachusetts Federation of Bee Keepers
Massachusetts Federation of Farmers Markets
Massachusetts Flower Growers Association
Massachusetts Fruit Growers Association
Massachusetts Lamb and Wool Board
Massachusetts Maple Producers Association
Massachusetts Nurserymen's Association
Massachusetts Poultry Association
Massachusetts Turkey Growers Association
Massachusetts Winegrowers Association
Milk Promotion Services, Incorporated
New England Vegetable Growers Association
New England Sprout Growers Association
New York-New England Apple Institute
Pioneer Valley Growers Association

FOREWORD

F resh. Flavorful. Distinctive. Just some of the words to describe the wonderful foods of Massachusetts.

Recipes For All Seasons captures the flavor, the spirit and the essence of Massachusetts in an innovative travel cookbook. It's chock full of recipes that showcase the wide variety of excellent Massachusetts-made products.

And it also provides a travelogue of scenic and historic Massachusetts as seen through the eyes of widely-read authors, Ruth and Milton Bass, Lynda Morgenroth and Anne Morris.

Produced by Leisure Time Publishing in cooperation with the Massachusetts Department of Food and Agriculture, this book offers both an armchair trip through the Bay State and a taste of its cuisine.

Recipes For All Seasons offers more than two hundred new reasons—with more than two hundred recipes—to use Massachusetts products every time you prepare a meal for family, friends and company.

Sit back and enjoy a taste of Massachusetts. We think you'll enjoy the trip.

Lynda Morgenroth, who writes here about three of her Massachusetts loves—Boston, the North Shore and Cape Cod, has lived in Boston for twenty-five years. She was born in New York and migrated to Boston during the sixties to attend art school. She left art, dabbled in film, but ultimately chose words "because they're small, neat, relatively peaceful and you can manage to live in Boston while working with them." Over the next twenty years she involved herself in writing for film, radio, newspapers and magazines.

During the last twelve years, Ms. Morgenroth has been a freelance feature writer for a variety of regional and national publications. She writes regularly on the New England cultural scene for *The Boston Globe* and *Yankee* magazine, on food and travel for publications such as *The New York Times, The Boston Phoenix* and *Bon Appetit,* and on social and medical issues for *The Atlantic* and *Ladies' Home Journal.* She teaches Essay Writing at the Boston Center for Adult Education.

NORTH SHORE

First time visitors to New England often arrive expecting one homogeneous region: a sprawling six-state pasture interrupted by white steepled churches, waterfalls, houses with porches, and public buildings with columns, domes and clocks.

Well, no presumption could be more insulting to the state-proud citizens of the six New England states, who pride themselves upon their differences. Like much associated with independence in this region, pride of place can get carried to extremes.

It can be a big deal for a Bostonian to agree to lunch with a friend in Cambridge. It's five minutes from downtown Boston to Cambridge by car—ten minutes from Park Street to Harvard Square by "T" (public transit)—but, you see, there is this river in between (The Charles). And a different culture, and traditions, and anyway, Boston is the hub, and wouldn't you really rather come here . . .

But pride of place aside, you cannot argue with Mother Nature.

Geologically, we in New England are related, the glaciers having preceded political history. Massachusetts' fertile Pioneer Valley looks a lot like the Connecticut River Valley—in our neighbor state to the south—through which the same river flows.

And though living on Cape Cod is certainly special, the beaches of Massachusetts' South Shore start to look a good deal like Cape Cod as you get closer and closer to Buzzard's Bay. Cranberries—no respecter of political boundaries—grow just as naturally on Massachusetts' southeastern mainland as on Cape Cod.

And so it is with Massachusetts' rock strewn North Shore. It looks not like Boston, not like Cape Cod, or the South Shore, but like the craggy, virile coast of Maine.

It is a place of wondrous, clear light. The wild, cold, majestic Atlantic. Imposing cliffs, hidden inlets and coves. Near miraculous natural harbors and forests of lofty pines. A place made for fishing, trading, ship building. Inland from the shore, where river waters flow, a place for mills, transport of goods, manufacturing.

You may choose to imagine Boston as a fulcrum with one sort of beach to the south—that of the feminine, undulating shore. And another sort of beach to the north—that of the masculine, craggy, majestic coast.

If you look at a map of New England, you will see that New Hampshire has just thirteen miles of shoreline, meaning that Massachusetts' North Shore and the coast of Maine almost touch. Maine juts out more into the Atlantic, but clearly the Maine coast and that of Massachusetts North Shore are kin.

Which is fortunate indeed for residents of Boston who wish to quit the city and head for cliffs, bracing air, unspoiled beaches on the Atlantic— one a major flyway for migrating birds—and a legacy of what made New England great: cod, clippers, trade; smarts, thrift and perseverance.

The modern history of the North Shore and inland river cities of Lowell and Lawrence are linked, but dissimilar. The social and economic history of Boston's North Shore—the Atlantic coastline from Boston to Newburyport at the northeastern tip—is associated with the power of the sea; specifically the plentiful supply of cod, the main "sea crop" for generations, along with trade, both domestic and international, and the building of ships, particularly the legendary clippers. The tall, straight pine trees the early settlers found became the masts of ships.

While many European immigrants came to the region during the nineteenth century—Greek and Portuguese fishermen are particularly associated with the town of Gloucester—the North Shore was a Yankee bastion. In particular the traders and sea captains were Yankee and the owners of many of the fishing fleets. Big money was made, big houses were built. Many of Boston's preeminent cultural institutions—the Boston Museum of Fine Arts and Boston Symphony, among them—can trace their economic origins to the fortunes made by Boston Brahmin families in seafaring, ship building and trade.

In addition, during the late nineteenth century and early twentieth— the pre-income tax era of massive capital accumulation—the North Shore became the chosen spot for scores of fabulously wealthy families, both those secure in "old money," along with fabled entrepreneurs, political elites and robber barons. The shore's distinction as America's first summer resort earned it the sobriquet, "Boston's Gold Coast."

Industrialists such as H. J. Heinz, the Ketchup King, Chicago plumbing heir Richard Crane and steel magnate Henry Clay Frick built baronial castles on the coast and came and went in well appointed private Pullman cars. Boston society was amply represented by the Cabots, Lodges and Lowells, along with that liberated patron of the arts, Isabella Stewart Gardner, aka "Mrs. Jack."

For a charmed era between the Gay Nineties and the crash of 1929, the "Gold Coast" became a xanadu for the rich and famous, including members of the international elite and America's power elite—such as Theodore Roosevelt, Franklin Delano Roosevelt and Alice Roosevelt Longworth. Many of the mansions and estates these families and individuals created remain. Some have remained "in the family," others sold to the computer and advertising magnates of our own day, while still others such as the Crane Estate in Ipswich belong to private, nonprofit conservation and preservation societies and are open to the public.

Lowell and Lawrence, inland on the mighty Merrimack River, never saw such a gilded age. But there was energy aplenty here, of men, women and children—many of them exploited before the rise of the American labor movement—and the enterprise of inventors and entrepreneurs. The place of Lowell and Lawrence in Massachusetts history, indeed American history and international labor history, is associated with the mills, mainly textile, which made Massachusetts and New England the manufacturing hub of the nineteenth and early twentieth century. During their nineteenth century heyday, these mill towns attracted immigrant workers from around the world—Greeks, Italians, Irish, Jews, Poles, French and Portuguese.

They brought not only their language, customs and religious beliefs, but also their food and celebrations. Lowell in particular has always been a place of entry for immigrants and continues to be so. Greek food, festivals and restaurants remain, along with the vestiges of many other nineteenth century settlers, but today the streets of Lowell are dominated by Southeast Asian and Hispanic people. The outdoor market features lemon grass, ginger and *cilantro* (Chinese parsley). Lively grocery stores stock plantains, the banana-like fruit that becomes ambrosia when breaded and deep fried, and *cassava* (the nutritious root from which tapioca is made), also deep fried and served with a delectable, colorful sweet and sour carrot sauce.

As with any series of contiguous, well established cities and towns, you can chart social history by shopping in town centers and keeping your eye on local festivals. Though Ipswich is often associated with Yankee descendants, particularly those of nautical lineage, the local Hellenic society stages its annual outdoor festival in Ipswich. The spirited, celebratory event features Greek music, dancing, performance and an array of culinary specialties—sizzling grilled kabobs, succulent eggplant casseroles and elegant filo-based desserts. Sitting at a little outdoor table, feasting on souvlaki, fresh feta cheese and briny olives, with a glass of retsina, you can fancy yourself in a taverna somewhere in the Aegean.

You can find Portuguese bread and soups on the menu of small eateries throughout the North Shore, and perhaps the most impressive and welcome cross fertilization of all, the influence of Mediterranean cooking on cod: turning it from a generic, crumb coated baked fish—morally upright but dull—to a delectable grilled item, laced with garlic and olive oil, festooned with sauteed onions, peppers, tomatoes.

In down-home restaurants in Salem, Gloucester and Rockport, you may even find homey dishes featuring baccala or *bacalhau*— cod that is salted and dried, then rinsed and reconstituted and miraculously fresh—a legacy of the Portuguese fishermen that did the hard work (and the best fishing, some say) in the pre-Frigidaire era when salt, not electricity, preserved fish.

You have a lot of choices in making a tour of Massachusetts' North Shore. You can head straight to Newburyport, the clipper capital and birthplace of the Coast Guard, at the northeasterly tip of the state, or spend your time on the peninsula of Cape Ann, where artists such as John Sloan, Edward Hopper and Childe Hassam were captivated by the air, the sea and the light.

You could fashion a kind of old fashioned motoring holiday, ambling along the coastline from Boston to Cape Ann to Newburyport, then inland to Lawrence and Lowell.

(You will have to suspend some disbelief with this route, especially on the Route 1 stretch just outside Boston, which traverses a jumbled path of motels; discount mattress stores; nightclubs of questionable artistic value; the largest Chinese restaurant in New England; a steak house with life size, grazing, plaster Holstein cattle; a miniature golf set-up and a gargantuan green dinosaur, the purpose of which we have never been able to construe. You will eventually pass this and reach beautiful winding roads with canopies of oaks and elms.)

An inspiring lesson in American history could be yours with a few days touring the city of Lowell, its vintage nineteenth century factories and navigable urban canals. Or combine the cultural and marine heritage of Newburyport with a visit to its celebrated barrier beach. Or head for

the beaches, fried clams and fine antiques of Essex, Ipswich and Gloucester. It's up to you.

If you made your way north from Boston, here's something like what you would find, complete with the requisite green dinosaur on Route 1:

You will first pass on the edge of Revere, still urban, and with a Coney Island type of beach—Boston's "phoney Coney" that served generations of working class Bostonians who needed a draught of fresh sea air. The boardwalk is still there, amusements, cotton candy, honky tonk and a people-intense urban beach scene. The commercial part of Revere has some of the best Italian restaurants in the city—with much better prices than those of the neighboring North End—and bakeries where the biscotti are fresh and crisp and they don't scrimp on the almonds. Revere's bakeries are also good places to buy pasta, some imported and with excellent "bite," some fresh, just waiting for a moment's closely watched immersion in boiling water and a toss of garlic and oil.

Lynn, "Shoe City," was once the world's leading producer of fine shoes, attracting shoemakers from all over the world. Today, the city's industrial and economic history is commemorated in Lynn Heritage State Park, a downtown esplanade with a view of Lynn Harbor, Massachusetts Bay and the Boston skyline. Like seven other Heritage State Parks in Massachusetts, Lynn's urban park is considered a national model of urban environmental planning. These parks, which include Lowell Heritage State Park and Lawrence Heritage State Park, are designed to celebrate a city's heritage, encourage private development, create outdoor urban spaces and bring people accustomed to shopping in malls and "mallettes" back into the downtown.

Northeast of Lynn, the sparkling upscale yachting town of Marblehead awaits. Everyone seems to have their own favorite view of Marblehead's fabled harbor—views by air, land and sea—but a particularly lovely one is from Crocker Park, a fine place for a picnic made from gourmet sandwiches, goodies and cakes gathered from one of the town's epicurean take-out places. Marblehead offers historical museums, a vibrant art center and pleasures for birdwatchers and walkers-down-

Brookline Farmers Market

country-lanes. A leisurely walk through the twisted small scale streets of the Old Town section will bring you past charming rose covered cottages and refined Federal-era houses, well stocked antique and curiosity stores, distinctive jewelers and unusual boutiques.

In addition to its singular status as a yachting center and its attractions for architecture buffs, Marblehead may be the street eating capital of New England. This is a bad place to visit if you're on a diet. In all weather, at all times of year, diverse citizens of Marblehead, or visitors celebrating sensory pleasures, are engaged in eating as they window-shop. Homemade ice cream in homemade cones, oatmeal raisin cookies with chunks of toasted walnuts, aromatic spinach pies with bits of feta cheese and pine nuts; these are a few of our favorite Marblehead comestibles.

At the end of the day in Marblehead, if you wish to withdraw from the bustle and sunshine of the town, stroll through the small, silent Mass. Audubon sanctuary on Risley Road, the last bit of wild land on Marblehead Neck. Giant maples and papery white birch fill the swampy woods and you'll find wild roses and blueberries in summer. If you own binoculars, this is the place to bring them. Over 235 species of birds have been sighted in this fifteen-acre haven.

Salem, the next town on your coastal migration, also has an urban look. But leave the beaten path and you'll find a handsome Federal-era town with beautifully preserved eighteenth and nineteenth century houses, a legacy of nautical and literary accomplishment, and the eerie, disturbing chapter of the seventeenth century Salem Witch trials.

While not overlooking the seriousness of these repeated incidents of persecution and suppression, the citizens of Salem decided some years ago to not only grin and bear their appellation of "Witch City," but to showcase it. The infamous witchcraft trials of 1692 are the subject of inquiry in the Salem's Witch Museum, Witch House (where one of the trial judges lived and also the site of preliminary hearings) and the Rebecca Nurse House, home of one of the convicted unfortunates.

A less despicable aspect of New England history can be seen at

Salem's Essex Institute: six sterling and intriguing preserved houses that represent New England architecture from the colonial through Georgian and Federal periods.

The Peabody Museum of Salem is really two museums in one. As the eighteenth and nineteenth century seafaring men of Salem dominate town history, the museum is, first of all, an excellent maritime museum with imaginative displays on navigation and maritime trade. But secondly, more artistically, are its treasures: the foreign goods and oriental exotica the sea travelers and traders brought back. The museum is nationally known for its holdings in oriental art, anthropological studies and decorative arts.

Salem's Heritage Trail, a self-guided walking tour, links thirty-historic sites, including Salem Common, the Essex Institute, Old Town Hall and several historic houses. Derby Street is a showcase of Federal-style houses and Salem Maritime National Historic Site, nine acres of historic waterfront.

Literati and lovers of old houses and gardens mustn't miss the House of the Seven Gables, inspiration for Nathaniel Hawthorne's atmospheric novel.

And in a contemporary, culinary vein, lovers of fine chocolate might consider an on site inspection and tasting at Harbor Sweets, the primo small-scale producer of fine chocolates in New England. In this friendly *chocolaterie* on Leavitt Street in Salem, the fabled sloop shaped chocolates are produced, along with confections in the shape of starfish and periwinkles. The shapes, though fetching, are secondary to the taste: the unexpurgated genuine article that brings exhilaration, exaltation and inner peace to chocoholics.

Harbor Sweets is open for tours and its products can be purchased in glossy red paper boxes in gourmet and gift stores throughout Massachusetts. The Sweet Sloops combine dark chocolate, white chocolate and buttercrunch. (A member of our family insists they are the definitive eighth food group, containing vital, if little known, nutrients.)

The nearby towns of Beverly, Hamilton and Wenham are "horse

country." The perimeters of groomed estates, parks and old pasture-land—much of it associated with "old money" and the North Shore's gilded era—are ideal for horseback riding. Polo is played at the prestigious Myopia Hunt Club in Hamilton, where British royalty still comes calling. Further inland, the historic villages of Georgetown, Boxford and Topsfield arc also "horse country" and rolling farm terrain. Topsfield is the site of the nation's oldest country fair, a spectacle not to be missed each fall—with quality entertainment, livestock shows, displays of epicurean delights and prizes awarded to the largest pumpkin (we are talking behemoths, in excess of 200-pounds).

Foliage lovers, please note, the backroads of "horse country" make fine fall foliage viewing, as do Routes 133 and 1A in their more northerly stretches.

Head inland to the pretty suburban town of Andover. Visit the Addison Gallery of American art on the landscaped campus of Philip's Academy, one of the finest preparatory schools in the United States.

In North Andover, the Museum of American Textile History illustrates the manufacture of woolen cloth, once a leading industry in the area.

Onward to Cape Ann, that jutting peninsula northeast of Salem, stretching to the sea. The peninsula begins inland in the south at Manchester and Magnolia, in the north at Ipswich and Essex, with the most easterly bits of this ocean empire in the fishing villages of Gloucester, Rockport and tiny Annisquam.

The seaside town of Manchester was the North Shore's first summer resort, where proper Bostonians gathered during the 1840s. Its elegant town center and picture-perfect Singing Beach continue to allure. You can pack up an old straw bag (not too old as this is a tony town), take a train from Boston and walk a few tree shaded blocks to Singing Beach. (Its name comes from the particular qualities of the sand. It's so hard packed that the scrape of a toe is said to produce a clear, musical tone.) The nineteenth century qualities of Manchester, the picturesque sym-metry of the beach and the pleasant pace of the North Shore train cohere well. A good nineteenth century novel and thermos of homemade lemon-ade (New Englanders like it tart, not sweet) would complete a day's idyll.

Follow the rugged shore northeast on Route 127 to Magnolia. Explore intriguing, if overstuffed Hammond Castle, built by inventor John Hays Hammond, Jr., who had a passion for medieval furniture, architecture and design. IIis castle, built from 1926 through 1928, incorporates portions of European houses and churches and has a fine 10,000-pipe organ, used for sonorous public concerts.

Onward to the craggy windswept tip of Cape Ann, where the light has a particular clarity and the air itself seems charged. Gloucester, the largest town on the North Shore, continues to be a world recognized port. The town's bustling waterfront is a pleasure for photographers, and the annual Blessing of the Fleet, a religious festival turned community and civic event, is a special time to go. It takes place each summer.

Gloucester has a lot of soul. Founded in 1623, it is the second oldest settlement in New England. Many of the settlement's early fishing fleet became vessels of war during the American Revolution. It is still a working port. Fish are processed on its docks. Thc town is dynamic, spirited and real— fishing vessels coming in and going out, catch being unloaded and the glorious sight of hundreds of lobsters in traps and the banter and hard work of the fishermen.

This is not the town for white tablecloths, fussy crustacean dissection implements and lobster in dainty casseroles. This is a place to 'rastle with the critters on scarred wooden tables outdoors, where you wear your old clothes and are up to your arms in bright red beast, plunging walnut-sized pieces of succulent, pure white lobster meat into your waiting craw. Melted butter will definitely run down your wrists.

Not only in summer, but through Indian summer and autumn, folks linger on the decks of local restaurants savoring *Homarus americanus*. In winter there's no let-up. They're still eating lobster, now indoors behind picture windows that frame the sea, followed by heavy mugs of strong coffee and big slices of apple pie made from the produce of North Shore orchards.

Gloucester's town piers are the launch site for whale watch excursions and the salty wharves of East Gloucester are host to a venerable artists colony. Check out the Gloucester Stage Company, also in East Gloucester, known for its critically acclaimed productions of new works. Long Harbor, Good Harbor and Wingaersheek are among the best beaches in the area.

In spite of the presence of seafood restaurants, an art colony and performing arts groups, all attractive to outsiders, Gloucester has maintained the bustling, clamorous quality of a real fishing town because of the continuing presence of its fleet and local fishermen, many of Italian and Portuguese descent. Rockport, a fishing village turned artists colony, has a more self conscious beauty, relying as it does on various classic scenic outposts, much documented by painters and photographers, and harbor walks.

Bearskin Neck, Rockport's signature shopping and gallery pier, leads you past shops and galleries galore, none exhibiting what you'd call great works of art, but enjoyable nevertheless.

Annisquam, off the beaten track on Ipswich Bay, is a small jewel, a tiny perfect fishing village now taken up by yachting pursuits. It looks like all our fantasies of New England-on-the-sea come true.

Ipswich north of Cape Ann is known for beautiful beaches, savory fried clams and restored seventeenth and eighteenth century houses, including Whipple House, furnished in period fashion and with an enchanting seventeenth century garden. This very special garden was poetically and knowledgeably restored by the late landscape historian, gardener and author, Ann Leighton.

Crane's Beach Reservation in Ipswich is considered by many sand, sky and surf connoisseurs to be the best on the North Shore. It is particularly prized by artists, and for many years Boston's best (and most irreverent) architects and designers met on the beach for an annual sand castle competition. What works of art were produced—ziggurats and neo-Habitats—only to be whisked away by the sea!

Nearby Goodale Orchards on Argilla Road is a charmed spot, a family run, one hundred-acre apple orchard and farm where produce and baked goods are sold from a vintage barn. Hayrides are offered in warm weather and you're free to roam amid the farm animals.

Most important, Goodale produces cider doughnuts before your eyes. These are impossible to describe. You have to be there, eating, eyes closed, concentrating. You will never eat one, and may eat six. These are simple, straightforward affairs, small, undusted, unfrosted, cinnamony and redolent of fragrant apple cider. As might be expected, the best possible chaser to these doughnuts is Goodale's own apple cider, which is amber colored, contains no preservatives and is made on the premises. Fall is the best time to mosey in here, when the maples have turned scarlet, leaves crunch underfoot and the aromas of hot cider and freshly made doughnuts mix with the salty sea air.

A slightly batty but ultimately civilized custom is to have your doughnuts around 11a.m. (energy for the day), and again around 4 p.m. (teatime) and then head for Woodman's.

Let us now talk bivalves. Even though nearby Essex is a decidedly attractive town, with a shipbuilding museum and river causeway, and antique stores that will make you long to collect, it is a certain bivalve that put Essex on the map.

We address the legacy and continuing popularity of the succulent, deep fried clam. You can have it at other places, but there's something about Woodman's, a roadside tradition on Route 133. Not only are the fried clams tender and aromatic, but you get to eat like a slob. Plus, Woodman's is history.

As the story goes, the very concept of the fried clam, began here. Clams are nothing new in the New England diet. They were a staple of the Native American diet. But on a hot summer afternoon in July of 1916 restaurateur Lawrence Woodman was grousing about business and how slow it was. He was grousing while frying potato chips. Business was down, he told a fisherman buddy of his, joining him over the splattering skillet.

"Why not toss some clams in with those chips?" suggested the buddy.

Woodman did. The rest is history. Woodman created the first fried clam in recorded history and climbed to new heights of entrepreneurial invention with the introduction of the fried clam platter. We are talking about a trio of off-the-Pritikin delicacies, friends: tender, crisp and yes, greasy, deep fried clams, deep fried onion rings, and suitably sauteed french fries. They're still lining up at Woodman's, Route 133, Essex. In warm weather, you can gobble your clams outside. In winter, Woodman's is like a steam bath, all the better to inhale pure unadulterated essence of fried clam. The fragrance will linger on your coat for days!

Lots of great antiquing in Essex, too—over sixty dealers in a one-mile stretch of Route 133 and hilly roads ideal for biking or a jog, which should not be attempted after supping at Woodman's.

There are other sources of protein nearby. Turkey farms, for example, which attract both old fashioned and new fangled cooks who insist on getting their Thanksgiving and Christmas birds fresh. Boundary Farm in Essex sells fresh or roasted birds, plus turkey pies, soups and stews. The main house on their property was built in 1686.

More farm finds: In recent years small, carefully controlled farmsteads producing a variety of delectable cheeses—cheddars, camemberts, goat cheeses—have evolved in Massachusetts, replacing European imports in some of Boston's best restaurants. Craigston Cheese Co. in Wenham south of Ipswich, for example, makes mold ripened soft camembert from luscious Jersey cow milk. Look for these small producers throughout the state—some are open for informal touring—and for Massachusetts cheeses in gourmet and health food stores, and on the menus of better restaurants. These lovingly produced cheeses are distinguished by a fine velvety texture and carry a range of flavors and subtleties supermarket cheese bricks never approach.

From Ipswich, you can make your way to Newburyport on bucolic Route 1A or the less lovely but faster Route 1. In summer and spring, Route 133 is a verdant winding road past pastureland, grazing cattle and sheep, antique-filled barns offering various "finds" and farm stands offering fresh picked produce, homemade jellies, jams of local wild berries and home-baked bread.

Newburyport, at the Commonwealth's northeasternmost tip, is a place to clear your head, raise your spirits and walk, walk, walk. The heritage of the city—the sea and what it brought and wrought—is everywhere. Its impact is apparent from the moment you approach from the outskirts where boatyards and taverns still stand, to when you enter the shipshape downtown—graceful three-story brick buildings and white church spires—to the geographic end, the barrier island of Parker River National Wildlife Refuge, which locals call Plum Island.

The prosperity that shipbuilding, trading (and let us not omit privateering—the freelance capturing of enemy ships) brought is attested to by the handsome Federal-style houses that line High Street, the historic district, along with the lush oriental rugs, finely wrought silver, featherlight china and opulent furniture that wealthy traders, travelers and investors were able to afford. These are all visible and accessible in collections of local house museums, notably Cushing House. A recently opened state park—a former North Shore estate, 500-acre Maudslay—is a near lyrical vantage point on the Merrimack River, a mix of nature and the landscape gardener's art.

In downtown Newburyport, the past and present deftly connect in the form of Waterfront Park, a splendid new park on the banks of the Merrimack River where the city began. From Waterfront Park, the clippers once sailed, the "largest, fastest, finest sailing ships in the world," according to a riverside monument. At Newburyport's water-front there is always the piercing, jubilant sound of circling herring gulls, the rhythm of the working boats coming in and going out and the ubiquitous red brick of the town's main buildings, all constructed of ballast carried in the hulls of the clippers.

The superb crafts in local shops—scrimshaw, silver, handmade clothing in cotton, silk and wool, jewelry, ceramics and even handmade books—are reminiscent of what has always been valued in Newbury-port: industry, dignity, beauty and craft.

In any time of year, reserve your keenest observations for Parker River Wildlife Refuge, one of just two barrier islands in Massachusetts, a haven for beach lovers, naturalists, birders and those of poetic temperament. Inhale the air, scan the horizon, examine the rich surrounding marshland and you'll sense the life that nourished the thoughts, spirit and industry of generations of citizens of Newburyport.

Inland from Massachusetts' North Shore is the region known as the Merrimack River Valley, the birthplace of America's nineteenth century Industrial Revolution. First settled as farming villages in the 1600s, these towns became centers of fishing, shipping and trade. In the early nineteenth century, the water of the Merrimack River was harnessed, providing power for factories and mills. Lawrence, "The City of Workers," became one of the greatest producers of woolen textiles in the world. Lowell, "City of Spindles," was a leading textile manufacturing center and America's first planned industrial center.

Lowell was named for visionary entrepreneur Francis Cabot Lowell, the canny Boston industrialist who memorized the structure of the British power looms in 1810 and recreated a cotton cloth factory, the first in America, in Massachusetts.

The city looks like what it was, and is: a red brick mill city, the base for eight major textile mills by 1836, and a thriving modern city with new houses, apartments, and Victorian houses that belonged to prosperous mill owners now converted to condos for hi-tech workers. With the dwindling of manufacturing in Massachusetts, Lowell, like many other mill towns, fell on hard times. It was rescued and revitalized by the creation of Lowell Heritage State Park—a formidable, fascinating and historically impeccable restoration of the old factories and mills, combined with social history exhibits and films—and the presence of Wang Laboratories, a leading hi-tech enterprise.

Today, the city boasts a lively art scene at the Merrimack Repertory Theatre, Lowell Memorial Auditorium and the University of Lowell. The "history telling tours" offered by Lowell's National and State Parks are another draw. You can travel by barge through the city's canals, trolleys and on foot to learn about the factories, mills, "mill girls," evolution of the American Labor movement and innovative system of power canals.

Members of the Beat Generation, or Beat wannabees, visit Lowell for other reasons. Jack Kerouac, whose legendary *On the Road* was the Bible of the Beat Generation, was born in Lowell in 1922 and grew up here. He is memorialized in a commemorative sculpture in Eastern Canal Park in downtown Lowell. Periodic walks and talks on the author are offered by the Lowell Historic Society and his gravesite at Edson Cemetery is also a pilgrimage point.

Visitors also throng to the New England Quilt Museum, the only museum of its kind on the East coast, a glorious, celebratory space with antique and contemporary quilts, a library, touring exhibits, lectures, workshops and a delightful shop.

The social history of Lawrence, south of Lowell, is similar to that of Lowell. During 1912, the year of the landmark textile workers' "Bread and Roses" strike, over 74,000 of Lawrence's population of 86,000 were immigrants, or the children of immigrants, mainly employed by the mills.

Lawrence Heritage State Park, another of the Commonwealth's successful urban site renovations, is in an 1840s former mill boarding house on the canal. Its two floors of compelling exhibits illustrate immigrant life and the "Bread and Roses" strike. The Bread and Roses Festival in Lawrence commemorating the strike happens every Labor Day weekend.

Lowell's immigrant heritage is celebrated each July in a massive three-day joy-riot on stages, in parks, in piers, all over the city. The event, the National Folk Festival— the oldest multicultural celebration in the United States—is a "biggie" on the folk festival circuit.

If you have a taste for the exotic and a love for your fellow being, this folk festival is a good time to show up. In years past, the festival showcased the music of the bayou, Appalachia, cowboys and Native Americans. They're all still represented, of course, but so are the people of Southeast Asia, who've come to dominate downtown Lowell. They are there in performance, in art works—magnificent embroidery and complex, vividly colored "story quilts"—but most of all in food.

Like the Greeks, Irish, French, Jews, Portuguese and Spanish before them, the 26,000 people from Cambodia, Laos, Vietnam and Thailand now living in the area have imported their homeland via cuisine. Lemon grass, chili peppers, lime leaves, curry, coconut milk, peanuts, tamarind, cilantro and basil are all employed in their seductive cuisines. The National Folk Festival is an ideal occasion to graze on Thai rolls, Pad Thai (rice noodles fried with egg, meat, scallions, bean sprouts and ground peanuts) and subtle, delicate Chicken with Lemon Grass.

If you miss this or other festivals, don't worry. A dozen restaurants in the area now serve Southeast Asian food, and the appealing ingredients can be found in grocery stores in Lowell's crowded urban enclave. The people, of course, are everywhere, adding to the population mix of descendants of nineteenth century immigrants and the young professionals and families who work in hi-tech. The karma of Lowell, this place of entry for immigrants, battered survivors with energy and dreams, goes on, its present incarnation crowded, brightly colored, redolent of ginger, lemon grass and the comforting aroma of steaming sticky rice.

APPETIZERS & SNACKS

Standing watch on lobster pots, Gloucester

Spicy Dip

1 (10 oz) pkg frozen chopped spinach, thawed	• Squeeze water out of thawed spinach.
1 (8 oz) can water chestnuts (optional)	• Finely chop water chestnuts.
1 (16 oz) ctn Czepiel's Sour Cream	• Mix all ingredients until thoroughly blended.
3 tbsp East India Instant India Curry Paste	• Makes 3-4 cups.

Shrimp Dip

10 large Icybay Salad Shrimp	• Puree shrimp in blender or in food grinder.
¼ cup Cains Mayonnaise	
hot pepper sauce	• Add mayonnaise, hot sauce and onion; salt and pepper to taste.
1 tsp grated onion	
salt and pepper	• Add cream until desired dipping consistency.
Cooper's Hilltop Farm Light Cream	• Makes 1 cup.

Wicked Awesome Bull Dip

1 cup Dixie & Nikita's Wicked Awesome Barbecue Sauce	• Mix barbecue sauce and cream cheese.
1 (8 oz) pkg cream cheese, softened	• Serve with potato chips, nacho chips, crackers or raw vegetables.
potato chips, nacho chips, crackers or raw vegetables	• Makes 2 cups.

Stuffed Quahogs

6 medium quahogs (hard shell clams)
1 tbsp chopped onion
1 tbsp chopped fresh parsley
1 tbsp olive oil
6, ¼" slices Carando Pepperoni, skinned
2 slices Sunbeam White Bread
quahog broth and shells
paprika

- Wash quahogs with stiff brush. Cook in ½" water until they are all open. Remove from heat; set aside and let cool in broth.
- Saute onion and parsley in olive oil 2-3 minutes.
- Remove meat from quahog shells; grind with pepperoni.
- Add to first mixture in skillet.
- Soak bread in remaining broth; squeeze out excess liquid, then add bread to mixture. Blend well.
- Spoon mixture into shells, sprinkle with paprika; bake 15-20 minutes at 350 degrees. Stuffing should be crusty on top but moist on the inside.
- Makes 12 half-shell stuffed quahogs.

Chips and Shrimp

2 lbs Campeche Marisol Shrimp
Tri-Sum Potato Chips

Marinade:
2 cups La Spagnola Corn Oil
1 tbsp salt
4 tbsp ketchup
1 tsp paprika
2 cloves garlic, chopped
1 tsp Worcestershire sauce
dash hot pepper sauce

- Mix together all marinade ingredients.
- Marinate shrimp 2-4 hours.
- After marinating, place shrimp in shallow pan.
- Pour half the sauce over shrimp, but do not cover.
- Broil at 350 degrees until lightly brown.
- Turn and broil other side.
- Serve on potato chips.
- Makes 20 appetizers.

Sesame Hoomus

1 (20 oz) can shelled chick peas

5 tbsp sesame tahini paste

1 lemon, juiced

2 cloves garlic, finely chopped

1 tbsp finely chopped onion

¼ tsp cumin

Venus Armenian Thin Bread or
Cracker Bread

- Drain chick peas, reserving half of liquid; place peas in blender or food processor.
- Add sesame tahini paste, lemon juice, garlic, onion and cumin; blend until pureed, adding chick pea liquid to desired consistency.
- For best results, refrigerate overnight.
- Spread on bread.
- Makes 2½ cups.

Chicken Almond Spread

2 cups ground, cooked chicken

½ cup ground New England Natural
Bakers Tamari Almonds

½ cup Cains Cholesterol Free Reduced
Calorie Mayonnaise

salt (optional)

bagel chips

paprika

- Combine chicken and almonds with mayonnaise to spreading consistency.
- Add salt, if desired.
- Spread on chips and garnish with paprika.
- Broil until lightly brown.
- Serve immediately.
- Makes 45-50 appetizers.

Green Chili Hors d'Oeuvres

12 Bent's Common Crackers

2 cups grated mild Cheddar cheese

2 tbsp chopped, seeded, canned
green chilies

- Split common crackers.
- Sprinkle with cheese; top with chilies.
- Bake at 425 degrees 5 minutes or until cheese melts.
- Makes 2 doz.

Blue Goat Cheese Hors d'Oeuvres

5 oz Westfield Farm Hubbardston Blue,
cut into wedges
or
7 oz Westfield Farm Classic Blue Log,
cut into medallions
1 loaf Roma French Bread

- Cut bread in half lengthwise.
- Place enough cheese on bread halves to liberally cover.
- Heat in 375 degree oven until cheese begins to melt, about 1 minute.
- To serve, cut into bite-sized cubes.
- Serves 30-40.

Peppered Ham and Cream Cheese

1 (8 oz) pkg cream cheese, at
room temperature
¼ cup horseradish
½ lb Carando Black Peppered Ham,
finely chopped
¼ cup crushed walnuts
Venus Whole Wheat or Rye Wafers

- Mix first 3 ingredients together in bowl. Shape into log or ball.
- Roll in crushed walnuts.
- Wrap in waxed paper or plastic wrap.
- Refrigerate 2-3 hours.
- Serve with wheat or rye wafers.
- Serves 12-16.

Baked Baby Gouda

14 oz Smith's Country Baby Gouda
1 (8 oz) tube crescent rolls

- Preheat oven to 375 degrees.
- Remove wax and thin yellow layer from baby Gouda.
- Remove crescent rolls from tube and unroll. When unrolled, the dough forms a rectangular shape. Do not separate into triangles.
- Place baby Gouda in center of rectangle.
- Bring long edges of triangle together; pinch to seal. Pinch together remaining edges of dough to completely enclose cheese.
- Place on cookie sheet; bake at 375 degrees 11-13 minutes, or until golden brown.
- Serve immediately.
- Serves 20-24.

Cheddar Fondue

2 (10.5 oz) cans Cheddar cheese soup
1 lb sharp Cheddar cheese
1 cup beer
1 tsp Worcestershire sauce
½ cup Sloan Tavern Honeysuckle Mustard
½ lb Blood Farm Bacon

- Cook first 5 ingredients in slow cooker on low 4-6 hours.
- Fry bacon until crisp. Drain; add to cheese by crumbling bacon.
- Makes 4 cups.

Cheese Puffs

2 egg yolks, beaten
1 tsp Worcestershire sauce
1½ cups grated Cheddar cheese
2 egg whites, beaten
½ cup finely crushed State Line Potato Chips
whole State Line Potato Chips

- Add egg yolks and Worcestershire sauce to cheese.
- Combine with egg whites; fold in crushed potato chips.
- Place small amount of mixture on whole potato chips; bake in 400 degree oven until puffed and brown, 5-6 minutes.
- Serve immediately.
- Makes 24-30 appetizers.

Parmesan Garlic Artichokes

1 (9 oz) pkg frozen artichoke hearts
1 doz Bent's Common or Water Crackers, split
¼ cup melted butter
¼ tsp garlic salt
dash pepper
3 tbsp Carando Grated Parmesan Cheese

- Cook artichoke hearts according to pkg directions; drain well.
- Slice artichokes in half; put cut side down on paper towels.
- Place 1 artichoke half on each split cracker; put on baking sheet.
- Mix together butter, garlic salt and pepper; drizzle evenly into crevices of artichokes and onto cracker.
- Sprinkle with cheese. Can stand, covered, up to 6 hours.
- Bake uncovered at 350 degrees 10 minutes.
- Makes 2 doz.

Over-Stuffed Mushrooms

24 large Delftree Shiitake Mushrooms
¼ cup melted butter
1 cup crushed Suncrisp Potato Chips
2 green onions, sliced
2 tbsp chopped parsley
2 tbsp Cains Cholesterol Free Reduced Calorie Mayonnaise
1 clove garlic, crushed
dash hot pepper sauce
paprika

- Remove and chop mushroom stems; set aside.
- Brush mushroom caps with butter.
- Arrange round side down on baking sheet.
- In bowl, combine stems, potato chips, onions and parsley; set aside.
- Mix mayonnaise, garlic and hot sauce. Toss with chip mixture; mound in mushroom caps.
- Dust with paprika.
- Bake in 375 degree oven 8-10 minutes until heated thoroughly.
- Makes 24 appetizers.

Pepperoni Pate

½ lb Carando Pepperoni, ground
½ cup butter, softened
1 tbsp drained capers
1 tbsp chopped green olives with pimentos
3 drops hot pepper sauce
½ tsp dry mustard
¼ cup Hood Whipping Cream
½ cup chopped parsley
Nejaime's Lavasch Crisp Wafer Bread

- Blend first 7 ingredients in blender until smooth.
- Spoon into crock or ramekin; sprinkle with parsley.
- Chill 2 hours or overnight.
- Serve with wafer bread.
- Makes 1½ cups.

Turkey Swedish Meatballs

2 lbs Mello Lane Turkey Farm
Ground Turkey

2 tbsp butter

⅓ cup finely minced onion

2 Pine Hill Farm Eggs, beaten

1¼ cups dry bread crumbs

1 tbsp chopped parsley

1 tsp salt

⅛ tsp pepper

½ cup Crescent Ridge Dairy Milk

½ tsp poultry seasoning

¼ cup La Spagnola Corn Oil

Sauce:

¼ cup all-purpose flour

2 cups hot water

1 tsp Worcestershire sauce

½ tsp salt

pinch cayenne

¾ cup Czepiel's Sour Cream

- Place ground turkey in large mixing bowl.
- Melt butter in small frying pan; add onion and saute until soft.
- Add onion and butter to turkey, together with eggs, crumbs, parsley, salt, pepper, milk and poultry seasoning.
- Mix thoroughly.
- Roll into small balls the size of cherry tomatoes.
- Heat oil in large frying pan over medium high heat; brown meatballs.
- Remove meatballs from pan but reserve oil.
- To make sauce, stir flour into oil remaining in frying pan.
- Place pan over medium heat; stir in hot water, Worcestershire sauce, salt and cayenne.
- Cook until smooth and thick; stir in sour cream.
- Return meatballs to pan; cook over medium low heat 20 minutes before serving.
- Serve in chafing dish with toothpicks on the side.
- Makes 36 meatballs.

BEVERAGES

Dawn breaks over Gloucester Harbor

Tea Cooler

4 cups water
4 tsp Barrows American Breakfast Tea
¼ cup sugar
1 (6 oz) can frozen lemonade concentrate, thawed
ginger ale
fresh mint

- In saucepan, bring water to boil.
- Turn off heat and add tea. Let steep, covered, 5 minutes.
- Strain tea while pouring into large pitcher.
- Add sugar; stir and cool.
- Stir in lemonade.
- Before serving, add ginger ale to taste.
- Pour in ice filled glasses.
- Garnish with mint.
- Makes 5½ cups.

Peach Tea

¾ cup iced tea
¼ cup Nashoba Valley After-Dinner Peach Wine
lemon slice

- In a tall glass, combine iced tea and peach wine.
- Add ice cubes and lemon slice.
- Serves 1.

Great Grape Iced Tea

9 lemon flavored herb tea bags
9 cups boiling water
1⅛ cups Welch's Purple Grape Juice
mint leaves and lemon slices to garnish

- Steep tea bags in boiling water 5 minutes.
- Remove tea bags. Stir in grape juice; chill.
- Fill tall glasses with ice, fill with tea.
- Garnish with mint and lemon slices.
- Makes 10 cups.

Apple Strawberry Refresher

2 cups Lincoln Apple Juice
2 tbsp Cumworth Farm Honey
10-12 fresh or frozen strawberries
mint sprigs to garnish

- Place all ingredients, except mint, in blender.
- Blend until all strawberries are liquefied.
- Serve in chilled wine glasses, garnished with mint sprig.
- Makes 2½ cups.

Grand Grape Granite

1½ cups Welch's Purple Grape Juice
1½ cups Lemon-Lime Slice
⅓ cup lemon juice
lemon twist

- Combine grape juice, soda and lemon juice in large pitcher; stir well.
- Place in freezer 2-4 hours, or until semi-frozen.
- Just before serving, stir to break up large ice crystals.
- Serve in chilled glasses, garnished with lemon twist.
- Serves 4.

Cranberry Holiday Punch

2 qts ginger ale
1 qt Mandarin Orange Slice
8 oz Lemon-Lime Slice
2 cups Ocean Spray Cranberry Juice Cocktail
orange slices and mint leaves to garnish

- Freeze 1 qt ginger ale in ice cube trays.
- Chill remaining soft drinks.
- When ready to serve, pour cranberry juice cocktail and carbonated beverages into punch bowl.
- Float ginger ale cubes.
- Garnish with orange slices and mint leaves.
- Serves 20-24.

Spiked Hare Punch

2 (2 l) btls Razcal Soda
1 (750 ml) btl rum
sliced limes, oranges and lemons
to garnish

- In large punch bowl, combine soda and rum.
- Float slices of lime, orange and lemon on top to garnish.
- Serve ice cold.
- Serves 25.

Hot Cranberry Cider

1 qt Carlson Orchards Apple Cider
1 (32 oz) btl Ocean Spray Cranberry
Juice Cocktail
½ cup lemon juice
⅓ cup firmly packed light brown sugar
8 whole cloves
2 cinnamon sticks

- In large saucepan, combine ingredients; bring to boil.
- Reduce heat; simmer, uncovered, 10 minutes.
- Remove spices.
- Serve warm.
- Makes 2 qts.

Sparkling Tea Punch

3 qts ginger ale, divided
1¼ cups sugar
1 cup hot water
1 cup lemon juice
3 cups Ocean Spray Orange Juice
1 cup pineapple juice
3 cups double-strength Barrows
Darjeeling Tea
1 (12 oz) can Razcal Soda
mint leaves

- Freeze 1 qt ginger ale in ice cube trays.
- Boil sugar and water 5 minutes.
- Combine with fruit juices and tea; chill.
- Just before serving, add thoroughly chilled soda and remaining ginger ale.
- Float ginger ale cubes and mint leaves.
- Serves 30-35.

GREATER BOSTON

The eternal verities of Boston come quickly to mind.

Boston is a city steeped in history, and politics, and commerce, with majestic, varied architecture, outstanding colleges and museums and public parks graced by statuary, monuments, swan boats, lagoons.

But there is another Boston, a more accessible, textural city on an everyday, usable scale. The grand buildings, squares and public monuments are here, of course, causing us to correct our posture and feel proud as we walk, but so are the homier, more earthbound aspects of the city—the food, markets, trees, people and neighborhoods that figure more in our lives than exactly how many statues there are on the Commonwealth Avenue Mall. (There are eight, beginning with Alexander Hamilton, ending with Leif Eriksson. The bronze of sailor-teacher-historian Samuel Eliot Morison is the best. Snow collects in the hood of his foul weather gear.)

Now, food may seem a funny thing to fix on, since after all, we are not

Paris. But look again. Carefully. Even at tarnished monuments and what may seem the mere dust of history.

Boston, established 1630, is a city that has various monuments to the codfish, including one kept in gleaming, polished condition in the gold domed Massachusetts State House. Massachusetts Bay was filled with them; they kept our ancestors alive.

This is a city known for its steamed brown bread, its soft-crusted Parker House roll and the custom of eating apple pie for breakfast ("What is pie for?" said philosopher Ralph Waldo Emerson to counter any nascent criticism of the custom.)

This is a place where early insurrection and the quest for liberty focused on the hurling of crates of tea into Boston Harbor. (It was black, aromatic, prized tea, but affixed with George III's ill-advised, unjust, untimely tax.) And where one of the great disasters of the twentieth century, the Great Boston Molasses Flood Disaster, took place when a ninety-inch tall metal tank of thick dark molasses burst at the seams in Boston's North End, coating the city with sugar for months and drowning a score of terrified North Enders, mainly Italian immigrants.

Boston is a city defined by the waves of immigrants who came bringing food, culinary customs and ingredients. Where the importing of spices—ginger, pepper, allspice and cloves—was considered essential. And where people have always liked their wine, their rum, their cider and beer.

For the culinary minded wanderer, bits of culinary history and mystery abound. Why, for example, do Bostonians eat so much ice cream, including all winter long? Why are we obsessed with lobster, featuring it in rolls, pies, bisques and stews?

Could a psychologist (or theologian, possibly) explain the profound pleasure, the virtual moral uplift, of old fashioned Saturday suppers of codcakes, coleslaw, baked beans and steamed brown bread? A Massachusetts senator once rose in the halls of Congress to extol the virtues of the codfish ball, equating their consumption (as leftovers) on Sunday mornings as an exemplification of Calvinist virtue (this during a debate on a pure food bill).

Is it not pleasing to consider that we've been eating puddings made of cornmeal, milk, eggs and molasses for centuries; that a variant of this recipe can be found in ancient cookbooks and that you can still walk into one of the city's older restaurants—Durgin Park, say, near Faneuil Hall, and order up a bowl? Topped with vanilla ice cream, which melts slowly, delectably, on the hot, satisfying pudding . . .

And isn't it satisfying to think of what the indigenous people of Massachusetts ate before we came—codfish, clams and game; cranberries; concord grapes; acorns, maize, maple syrup and watercress.

If you are observant, you will see today—in Boston's vacant lots and urban wilds, and on the Boston Harbor Islands—many of the plants used by Native Americans generations ago. Cranberries and blueberries and oak trees grow here, dropping the nutritious acorns we no longer use.

For generations before the coming of the colonists, the Indians of Massachusetts fished, hunted, planted, gathered. There were cranberries in the bogs, blueberries in the woods and sweet amber syrup from the sugar maple trees.

In the seventheenth century, the English colonists arrived, bringing trees, plants, poultry, cattle and swine from their villages. They brought their tastes for what we now call "comfort foods"—roasts, puddings and pies. Much later, in the waves of nineteenth century immigration, immigrants from Europe, Asia and central Europe swelled our population and enlarged our culinary repertoire. Freed black slaves migrated north. French families from Canada moved south.

These countless generations of eaters and cooks were aided by Massachusetts' fertile soil and the resulting bounteous yields of vegetables and fruit. Verdant meadows beside brooks and river beds provided acres of grazing land. The hay of salt marshes was good for fodder and fertilizer both. Salt from our coastal waters was used to preserve meat and fish. Herbs to flavor and disguise.

Bits of yeasty "starter," or leavening, were passed around, as were "receipts" for potages and porridges. Trees were tapped for syrup. Roots were boiled for tea. It was hard controlling the early hearth ovens in fireplaces and, later, wood stoves. It was hard to replicate measurements, too, but people ate, lived, enjoyed. Some people cooked better than others, then as now.

Fannie Merritt Farmer (1857-1915), born in Boston, made culinary history by inventing a scientific approach to cooking. Director of the Boston Cooking School, she introduced standardized level measurements in recipes. *The Boston Cooking School Cookbook,* first published in 1896, was revised twenty times in her lifetime and exists today as *The Fannie Farmer Cookbook,* a culinary classic. Her publisher, Little, Brown and Company, sits proudly and prominently today across from the Public Garden on Beacon Hill.

Food philosopher and crusader Sylvester Graham (as in graham cracker) had a major influence in nineteenth century Boston. His condemnation of fats, gravies, seafood and mass-produced white bread caused many Boston families to feature oatmeal, beans, rice and home baked bread on their tables. Though his faddism has been tempered by time, Bostonians developed a reputation for health consciousness, eating in moderation and relying where possible on locally grown and produced edibles.

Today, the produce of Massachusetts orchards and farms, the fish from our waters, the varied tastes and talents of our immigrants, the legacy of interest in "scientific cookery" and what has come to be called "Yankee ingenuity" have all combined to distinguish Massachusetts, and Boston in particular, as a culinary mecca.

You could travel around the world by eating in Boston restaurants, starting with foods of the Aegean and ending, if not at "Z," then at "Y" with a delectable red snapper served with pumpkin seed sauce at a Cambridge restaurant featuring specialties of the Yucatan. You can take serious cooking courses at adult education centers, colleges and institutes all over the city, or watch one of the many cooking programs on our local public television station, WGBH-TV. You might see Julia Child drive by, a long wooden spoon mounted on the hood of her car.

From June through November, you can shop at the farmers markets all over the city, including in the grand space between the Boston Public Library and Trinity Church, Copley Square.

The Commonwealth of Massachusetts has become known as a high quality, specialty food producer. Some of these food products are fancy— rarified poultry and exotic herbs grown especially for Boston's best restaurants. (Sometimes chefs and farmers work together, focusing on irresistible edibles portrayed in specialty seed catalogs.) There are vineyards in the Bay State, some of which make historically authentic fruit wines. These—blueberry, cranberry, peach—are the colors of stained glass windows and taste like the essence of sun ripened fruit.

There are small scale farmstead cheese producers, some making rich, smooth, elegant French-style camemberts that our colonial ancestors, with the possible exception of Ben Franklin, never dreamed of.

Some of these food products are unfancy. But tasty, because they're local. Maple syrup, milk, cranberries, corn. Just about any vegetable or fruit you would want to eat, and some that are hard to find. Old fashioned apples (ever had a Pippin, or a Paula Red?). Rhubarb, in season, that cooks up silky (very good with a sprinkle of ginger). Asparagus. Green peas. Boston lettuce. Tomatoes with taste.

Some of the state's products are manufactured, only logical in a region with agricultural and manufacturing roots. In the Boston area, we still make cookies, biscuits, candy, cakes and bread. We brew beer. We even have a restaurant where you can drink the beer that's made on site, along with accompanying and appropriate victuals. Then tour the brewery.

Bagels are baked all night in Brookline, Boston's "streetcar suburb" ten minutes from the downtown. Pizza's tossed in the air in the North End, the big round familiar shape and the rectangular, Sicilian-style. Spices are pounded for Indian curries. Rice neatly rolled in seaweed. Plump dumplings deep fried. And beans still slow-cooked in our ovens, and yes, brown bread in proper one-quart pudding molds—or coffee cans—on the back burners of our stoves.

Throughout the city of Boston, should you care to take a culinary-spiced tour, vestiges of the foods of our forebears remain, along with the contemporary Bostonian's fascination for beautiful, interesting, sustaining food. This is the home of the bean and the cod, it is true, but also of the pepperoni pizza (North End), spicy kibbie (South End), pad thai (Beacon Hill), baba au rhum (Back Bay), quesadilla (Jamaica Plain), onion bagel (Brookline), shrimp saag (Allston) and an astonishing array of tapas (Cambridge).

If you're expecting a staid, buttoned-up Boston, you're in for a surprise. Boston's colonial past is in evidence, but integrated with an innovative, sometimes controversial contemporary arts scene, some of the best architecture in the country, parklands that stretch from rolling Boston Common to the 265-acre Arnold Arboretum and a culinary apotheosis that's the talk of the nation. Six restaurant guides have come out completely devoted to Boston, thank you very much. That's *our* chef on the cover of the fancy cooking magazine, *our* bluefish with mustard sauce, *our* Indian pudding being presented as just the thing to "do" for Thanksgiving. And that old eatery we thought was *our* secret is being sanctified as The Source of Authentic New England on the national news.

("Hmmmf. Hope the prices don't go up. Hope they don't cram in more tables," is the reply of your average Bostonian.)

When you visit, expect eclectic combinations. You may tour Tory mansions, then lunch Thai-style. You are likely to follow the trek on the Freedom Trail, then break for cannoli, with your choice of custard or ricotta filling. While exploring the largest Victorian neighborhood in the nation, Boston's South End, you will pause for some amazing bistro cooking, or colonial cuisine with panache, or the best of contemporary American.

You will be smitten by the layers of the city, its hospitality, pleasures and good sense.

In color, Boston is ruddy, the hue of the red brick townhouses in the residential sections of the Back Bay, South End and Beacon Hill. In light, it is bright, thanks to the cleansing properties of the sea breezes and gusts—Boston is said to be windier than Chicago—and proximity to the sea. In size, it is compact, a walker's city and definitively not a good place to drive. In character, it is gracious and welcoming, in part because of the goodly amount of open space, including the Emerald Necklace, the chain of parks that stretches from the Boston Common to the outer limits of Franklin Park. Sprawling, naturalistic Franklin Park, the "crown jewel" of the Emerald Necklace, is considered the masterpiece of Frederick Law Olmsted, the great nineteenth century landscape architect and planner.

It is a city that encourages freedom, with not only parks to roam and squares to amble through, but with the murky but lovable Charles River running alongside. The Paul Dudley White bike paths follow the river—a boon for joggers, cyclists and urban naturalists—and you can spot the black crowned night heron from the banks of the Charles.

You can walk anywhere in Boston. You can dispense with your car. You are advised to. Our streets are narrow, made for people and cows, not cars.

For ordering purposes, you may consider Boston Common the hub. Though not actually the city's geographic center, several sections of Boston surround the Common. It serves as the starting point for the well trod Freedom Trail and it has ancient, venerable agricultural associations.

The Boston Common is the oldest public park in the nation, established as common grazing land by the Puritans soon after their arrival in 1630. Contented cows grazed its acres for decades and it has long been the city's symbolic gathering place. Concerts, demonstrations, declarations and gatherings of troops.

Each spring of late the region's dairy farmers and ice cream makers sponsor a charitable fundraiser featuring ice cream. For a week, usually in early June, cows return to Boston Common (they were officially banned in 1830) and booths are set up by various ice cream makers. Visitors play a flat fee and are free to eat as much ice cream as they wish. The air is mild, the cattle calm, and the ice cream very good. So is the mix of people—from State Street bankers in pinstripes, to college athletes in sweats, to throngs of excited children, to elderly couples sharing ice cream, discussing relative merits.

You have no doubt heard of the Freedom Trail and may imagine it a Disneyesque attraction with simulated sights. In fact, it is more prosaic, gritty and singular. It is a concept, a unifying device: the linking of sixteen of Boston's most historic outposts by a wide red line painted on the city's sidewalks, cobblestones and brick paths. The red line crosses streets, goes up some hills and continues for about three miles, guiding visitors past the American Revolution's most important sites in two to three hours. The Freedom Trail begins at the information booth on the Tremont Street side of the Boston Common.

The trail leads through Boston history, right past Boston today. Downtown, amid a maze of narrow streets that lead to the waterfront and many seafood restaurants, you'll find State Street and the small, but majestic Old State House, the seat of colonial government. You can view the adjacent site of the 1770 Boston Massacre, which was a prelude to the Revolutionary war. Old South Meeting House, where the Sons of Liberty planned the guerilla action known as the Boston Tea Party, is a few steps away. King's Chapel, the first Anglican church in America, can be seen on nearby School Street, along with one of the most majestic buildings in New England, Old City Hall.

Today, this stately French Second Empire building—one of many French-inspired buildings in Boston—houses an excellent French restaurant and cafe. In warm weather, tables are set up outside and you can lunch on French delectables beneath the sage gaze of Ben Franklin, whose statue graces the patio outside Old City Hall. Franklin represented the thirteen colonies in Paris and was much beloved by the French, who considered him the embodiment of the Enlightenment. He was born in Boston and his parents are buried in the old Granary Burying Ground, also on the Freedom Trail.

Since today's Boston overlays historic Boston, you may wish to deviate from the Freedom Trail now and then. Stray a block from the Old

State House to Washington Street and Downtown Crossing, a pedestrian mall in Boston's lively downtown shopping area with Filene's, Filene's Basement and the Jordan Marsh Company.

The Theatre District is a few blocks away, as is Boston's Chinatown neighborhood, a trove of restaurants, bakeries, groceries and Asian cultural events, including Chinese New Year celebrations. In the snazzier restaurants of Chinatown, you can have an elegant dinner. In the smaller, more modest restaurants, the food is often as good, or better, and the prices lower. Visit the grocery stores for well priced Chinese cooking implements and ingredients such as bean paste, hoisin sauce and star anise. At New Year's time, Chinatown's bakeries carry handsome cookies in the shape of animals, such as carp and shiny, browned Buddhas.

Here, too, are some of Boston's oldest, most esteemed restaurants— Locke-Obers on Winter Place a half block from Filene's, a magnificently paneled Boston institution with heavenly oyster stew; Jacob Wirth Company, a German restaurant on Stuart Street that serves a tradi-tional New England boiled dinner (skip it and order the lobster salad) and the Parker House at Tremont and School, home of the Parker House roll.

Return to the Freedom Trail and head for handsome, beautifully proportioned Faneuil Hall, first built in 1742, rebuilt in 1763 following a fire and for 150 years a place of commerce and historic debate, Boston's "Cradle of Liberty."

Just behind Faneuil Hall is Faneuil Hall Marketplace, which locals call Quincy Market ("Quinzee Mahket"), named for the long, low carefully restored nineteenth century granite market hall and its neighboring North and South markets. At night the striking architecture of these market buildings becomes apparent. Before adjacent land was filled, they were at the water's edge, receiving docks where the city shopped. These markets, conveying meat, fish, produce, grains, coffee and spices, fed Boston. Today, in daytime, the area becomes a virtual carnival teeming with shoppers and visitors who move through the food stalls, restaurants and stores and enjoy street performers and performing arts at Faneuil Hall. The echoes of eating and foreign ports, though gussied up in this prototypical urban mall, remain.

In concessions at Faneuil Hall Marketplace you'll find Greek, Chinese, Mexican and Middle Eastern food; bagels, pizza, bakeries, cheesecakes, chocolates and every imaginable edible.

You can take your selections to a table indoors, or bench outdoors, or just "graze," consuming your comestibles as you go.

You are also close to several ancient Boston restaurants—Durgin-Park across from Faneuil Hall, with its long family-style tables, tart tongued waitresses and serving astonishing quantities of stews, lobsters and scrod; Yankee pot roast, Boston baked beans and of course Indian pudding. Just outside the marketplace, The Union Oyster House at 41 Union Street serves every possible combination of lobster, scallops, scrod, cod, salmon, halibut, swordfish, haddock, bluefish and sole. And very good Indian pudding. The restaurant opened in 1826.

The Custom House, formerly a federal building that served the port of Boston, is visible from the rear of Faneuil Hall Marketplace. It was the city's first skyscraper, built between 1837 and 1847 at what was then the water's edge. The tower with clock was added to the original Greek Temple-looking structure between 1913 and 1915. To many Bostonians and visitors, this distinctive building with its grand lighted clock is the symbol of Boston, a monument to its maritime history and sentinel on the water—quirky, dignified, beloved.

Boston's waterfront is a mix of deluxe and for real, a place where you can watch the day's catch being auctioned (very early in the morning), or luxuriate in your leather lounge chair on the piazza of one of the high priced condos created from old wharf buildings. The harbor area just behind Quincy Market—a place of wharf buildings abandoned thirty years ago, thriving commerce a century ago—has been gentrified to the status of a Gold Coast. Both pleasure boats and fishing boats come and go, which you can watch from the grand dining rooms of several waterfront hotels, or from the rear windows of a popular no frills seafood restaurant, No Name, on Fish Pier off Northern Avenue.

A lot goes on at the Waterfront and, fortunately, there's a park to rest in and watch the passing parade—young professionals who've picked up their take-home suppers from local suppliers; Italian children from the nearby North End rushing home with breads, often with the end chomped off; smart shoppers riding by on bicycles with tell-tale butcher paper parcels—well priced fresh fish—in their baskets or poking out of rucksacks. Waterfront Park is a graceful open space with trellised plantings, a neighborhood center on the Boston Harbor.

There's treasure on every wharf on the Waterfront, and it isn't buried. Big seafood restaurants on the piers off Northern Avenue, the Computer Museum and Children's Museum on Museum Wharf (Congress Street), along with the Boston Tea Party Ship and Museum. The New England Aquarium on Central Wharf is famous for its sea lion and dolphin shows, whale watching expeditions and magnificent cylindrical viewing tank. (Visitors walk around it, on a spiraling ramp.) Rowes Wharf has a handsome hotel with fine restaurant, a ferry to Logan Airport, a delightful waterfront walkway completely open to the public and an outdoor cafe.

The piers along the Waterfront also serve as ports of call to cruise ships and ferry lines that take visitors to Provincetown on Cape Cod, Gloucester on the North Shore, the islands of Martha's Vineyard and Nantucket and the nearby Boston Harbor Islands, little worlds onto themselves.

Food, people, neighborhood—that's the North End in a nutshell, or perhaps we should say in a thin, crisp cannoli shell. This small, dense, neighborhood, once home to Irish immigrants, Boston's black population, and Jewish immigrants from central Europe, is now largely Italian, though increasingly, young professionals have bought condos in the area. The North End is the place to shop for pasta, veggies, sausage, mozzarella made in the back of the store and parmesan cut off a big, heavy, aromatic wheel. There are over a dozen places to buy Italian

bread—round ones, long ones, short ones—and cookies with whole almonds, toasted sesame seeds, *pignoli* (pine nuts) and luscious marzipan.

With its narrow streets, brick apartments and lively street life, this colorful neighborhood is one of the treasures of Boston—with bakeries, cafes, espresso bars, restaurants, specialty groceries and outposts of seventheenth, eighteenth, and nineteenth century Boston. Paul Revere's house, the oldest wooden building in Boston, is here, along with Old North Church, where two lanterns were hung in April 1775 to signal to the Patriots across the river that the British were coming ("one if by land, two if by sea . . .").

Nearby Copp's hill Burial Ground, used as a cemetery since 1660, is the burial place of stern Puritan preacher Cotton Mather and shipbuilder Edmund Hartt. The most famous—and probably most beloved—ship Hartt built, the *U.S.S. Constitution* ("Old Ironsides") can be glimpsed from Copp's Hill in its berth at the Charlestown Navy Yard. Launched in 1779 and undefeated in the War of 1812, "Old Ironsides" is the oldest commissioned warship in the United States Navy.

The Freedom Trail follows the edge of the North End to the Charlestown Bridge, off Commercial Street, and to the Charlestown Navy Yard, future site of the New England Aquarium. In breezy, bustling Charlestown Navy Yard, you can board "Old Ironsides" and visit an excellent nautical museum. The nearby Bunker Hill Monument commemorates the site of the first major battle of the Revolutionary War and is the stirring finale of the Freedom Trail.

Beacon Hill, at the Northern edge of Boston Common and the Public Garden, is one of the city's most venerable and valued neighborhoods. It is a place of impeccable townhouses, hidden gardens, cobblestone walks and shimmering gas lamps to light your way.

Charles Street, at the foot of "the Hill," is the elegant commercial center of the area. Lining the street are antique shops, bookstores, bakeries, galleries, boutiques and eateries. A block away, the Charles River runs parallel to Charles Street. In warm weather, the well used

Paul Revere and the Old North Church, Boston

waterway is dotted with sailboats and crew boats. Bikers, joggers, dog walkers and their Labrador Retrievers and Collies silhouette the water's edge, as do the tame mallards, making their way up the river bank.

This pastoral scene is the backdrop for free summer concerts in the Hatch Shell on the Esplanade. The Boston Pops perform an annual Fourth of July concert here, complete with fireworks and hundreds of thousands of revelers. Bostonians come early and stay late, bringing lavish picnic hampers with fancy sandwiches, cold chicken and exotic salads (Indonesian rice salad is in), P & J for the kids and berry pies and chocolate cakes that wind up being shared with strangers.

Uphill, the brick-faced residential townhouses of Beacon Hill were once home to literati such as William Dean Howells, editor of *The Atlantic*; Louisa May Alcott and her family; Julia Ward Howe, author of the "Battle Hymn of the Republic," and writer and critic Henry James.

The Black Heritage Trail winds along Beacon Hill's north slope, the neighborhood where nineteenth century black Bostonians lived. The Abiel Smith School, the first public school for black children in the country, is here. You'll also find the African Meeting House, the oldest (1806) black church building still standing in the U. S., and vestiges of the Underground Railroad, such as Hayden House, a former station.

The gold domed State House, masterpiece of architect Charles Bulfinch, rises above the Boston Common and Boston's downtown, crowning Beacon Hill.

You can stroll the Boston Common and the flower-filled Public Garden, where swan boats glide in the pond. A series of cast bronze statues stands in charming tribute to the children's classic *Make Way for Ducklings* by Robert McCloskey. The many statues in the Garden, American's first public botanical garden, commemorate great authors, statesmen and medical marvels, including the first successful use of ether in surgery at the nearby Massachusetts General Hospital.

In the Common, just across the way from the Massachusetts State House, is a tribute to the first black regiment, led by Colonel Robert Gould Shaw. The first regiments of freed blacks in the Civil War were formed in Boston. Shaw, the son of an idealistic Boston Brahmin family, died while leading the assault on Fort Wagner, South Carolina in 1868. The story of the regiments was chronicled in the 1989 movie "Glory." The bas-relief memorial, created with funds raised by a citizens' commission, was dedicated in 1897 after thirteen years work in the studio of sculptor August Saint-Gaudens. The monument stands between two ancient elms.

This splendid urban domain is called Back Bay because it was once under water.

Feast your eyes on the rectilinear order of this enclave, a neighborhood of handsome townhouses, century-old trees and carefully kept postage stamp-sized gardens, and it's hard to imagine. Yet what you see at the entrance to the Public Garden on Arlington Street is land that was filled over one hundred years ago. The Garden itself is filled land, as is majestic French-inspired Commonwealth Avenue and the lot that holds the Ritz-Carlton Hotel.

Commonwealth Avenue forms a wide, Parisian-style boulevard. Its central mall features magnificent wineglass-shaped American elms, sweetgums and zelkovas; ageless statues surrounded by evergreens, with red brick and cocoa-colored townhouses on either side. Newbury Street, New England's most exclusive shopping street, has scores of art galleries, deluxe jewelry stores, salons, haberdashers, designer fashion outposts, boutiques, specialty shops and restaurants. These run the gamut from elegant hotel restaurants such as the dining room at the Ritz-Carlton and Aujourd'Hui at the Four Seasons, to sleek contemporary Italian bistros—Davio's, Ciao Bella—to Japanese, Chinese, Thai, French, southwestern and eclectic contemporary American, the latter exemplified by the fashionable Biba on Boylston Street.

Boylston leads to Copley Square, a Back Bay crossroads of four beloved Boston buildings: noble Italian Renaissance-style Boston Public Library (BPL); granite and sandstone Romanesque-style Trinity Church, the masterpiece of architect H. H. Richardson; northern

Gothic-style Old South Church and the graceful limestone Copley Plaza Hotel.

These four buildings are worth a visit to Boston—the majesty of the BPL's second floor reading room overlooking Copley Square, and its courtyard; the massive rusticated stone of Trinity and the soaring space within; the bright colors and warmth of Old South and the two fine, friendly lions flanking the entrance of the Copley Plaza.

Imagine shopping for corn, tomatoes, broccoli, apples and blueberries surrounded by these buildings. That's what goes on a few times a week in warm weather when Massachusetts farmers set up their stands in Copley Square. Bostonians buy farm fresh produce in the company of gilded lions, gargoyles and so much stained glass. And we appreciate it when the farmer we've come to know throws some extras at us, including a recipe for Harvard beets.

Architecture and Harvard beets aside, Boylston Street is known to millions of runners as the finish line for the Boston Marathon, America's oldest. It's also the route of the spectacular December 31 parade that kicks off "First Night," Boston's gala, city-wide celebration of the arts. Thousands of performers entertain in theaters, recital halls, churches, museums, bank lobbies and even department store windows. Hot pretzels, hot cider and chestnuts are sold in the streets and revelers roam from event to event.

Nearby Copley Place is an indoor shopping pavilion with exclusive department stores, boutiques, shops and a cinema complex. For cooking mavens, it has several well stocked culinary implement and china stores—Williams Sonoma and Crate and Barrel, among them—with friendly, knowledgeable staff.

A mini-neighborhood, referred to by some as the "Avenue of the Arts," begins on Huntington Avenue in Copley Square. A short bus ride from the BPL brings you to the Boston Museum of Fine Arts, one of the great art institutions in the world; Symphony Hall, home to the Boston Symphony Orchestra and Boston Pops; The Huntington Theatre; and the New England Conservatory of Music, which offers free concerts by students and faculty almost every night of the year.

An easy walk across the grassy Fenway, part of the Emerald Necklace, brings you to the Isabella Stewart Gardner Museum, an extraordinary private collection of Italian and Renaissance art housed in a 1902 building styled after a fifteenth-century Venetian palazzo. (Imagine the stir Mrs. Gardner—Mrs. John Lowell Gardner, Jr., aka "Mrs. Jack"—made when she had her gorgeous, glorious house-museum built in dour turn-of-the-century Boston, and then commenced traipsing the world collecting art with the help of art historian Bernard Berenson. Her motto, *"C'est mon plaisir"* (It's my pleasure), offered in explanation of her voracious collecting and love of life was considered shocking, and un-Bostonian, as were her walking down Tremont Street with a lion on a leash and spending lavishly on jewelry and clothes. By all accounts, she had a wonderful life.

The interior courtyard of her museum is filled with flowers, neatly summing up Mrs. Jack's flair, generosity and taste. In winter, when the red, rose and magenta cyclamen bloom, it is most wonderful of all.

Back at the BPL, Dartmouth Street, which runs between the library and Copley Square, leads to the South End, the largest preserved Victorian neighborhood in the country.

The South End's vibrant arts community radiates from the Boston Center for the Arts at the corner of Berkeley and Tremont Street streets. There are several contemporary art galleries and a performance space in the Villa Victoria section on West Newton Street. The building of this neighborhood, also filled land, preceded the building of the Back Bay by about twenty years, beginning around 1835. A number of remarkable, oblong English-style parks remain and should be part of your walking tour.

Working class and immigrant residents began to live in the South End during the late nineteenth century. They included the young Lithuanian, art-historian-to-be Bernard Berenson, and Lebanese author and poet, Kahlil Gibran.

By the turn of the century, Irish immigrants had arrived, along with Jewish, Italian, Chinese, Greek, Syrian and Lebanese. Today the area is socially diverse, and largely gentrified, but with many traces of the people who once dominated this neighborhood lingering in restaurants, groceries and shops.

The South End is an eater's paradise, with numerous upscale bistros and cafes; Middle Eastern, soul food and Creole/Cajun spots and a wonderful breakfast place, Charlie's Sandwich Shop, operated by the same Greek-American family for over sixty years. On Shawmut Avenue there's a Middle Eastern grocery store where the bins of spices and burlap sacks of coffee beans and nuts draw you in from the street.

When snow blankets this sprawling neighborhood—its iron gates and vintage street lights, its many Victorian churches and small storefronts—it becomes eerily still, and magically, 1845.

The way Bostonians see it, Cambridge is our Left Bank. The way Cantabrigians see it, Boston is their Right Bank. Let us state the case directly:

The Charles River runs between Cambridge and Boston. Many Bostonians think of the Charles as Boston's Seine and of Cambridge as Boston's Left Bank. Cambridge is offbeat, zany and lovable. Thousands of students and scholars create an atmosphere of energy and excitement.

Many Cambridge-dwellers would probably say of Bostonians that we have a superior attitude, develop premature lines in our foreheads and stop after the second glass of wine. Which isn't true, but is why it is dangerous to lunch in Cambridge.

Cambridge is identified with its magnificent halls of learning. The best known are Harvard University, the oldest in the nation, and the Massachusetts Institute of Technology (MIT). Each has grand architectural presence, extensive libraries and a plethora of activities open to the public. The local entertainment scene is rich—jazz clubs, classical music, dance, comedy and innovative performance at the American Repertory Theatre.

Via the Red Line of the "T," Boston's public transit system, it's a snap to get from Park Street in downtown Boston to Harvard Square—the red brick cloisters, well trod lawns and majestic shade trees that compose Harvard Yard. Tours of the campus are available and you may want to visit Radcliffe's Schlesinger Library on the History of Women in America. This small, cozy library in Radcliffe Yard off Brattle Street is the largest women's history library in the country and welcomes visitors, including non-scholars. The library's holdings—everything from *Seventeen* magazine to the manuscripts of Amelia Earhart—include more than 3,000 cookbooks. Between the bindings of these cookbooks, a social history of America can be traced. Not to mention the definitive recipe for Indian pudding.

Harvard's outstanding museums are all located in the area—art museums (Busch-Reisinger, Fogg, Sackler), museums of natural history and the Harvard Semitic Museum. Harvard Square—perennially young—is dominated by bookstores, coffee houses, cafes, boutiques, ethnic restaurants, gourmet and kitchen supply shops, small department stores and movie theaters.

Meander out from the Square along Brattle Street to see Federal and Georgian-era mansions, and enormous shade trees. Stop at the Blacksmith House, established by refugees during World War II, for Viennese and French pastries, a good cup of coffee or comforting pot of tea. During the Revolutionary War era, Brattle Street, this enclave of prosperous Cantabrigians, was known as Tory Row. One of the grandest homes on the row served as George Washington's Revolutionary War headquarters in 1775 and was later the home of poet Henry Wadsworth Longfellow. Now known as the Longfellow Craigie House, it is a national park site, open for tours.

The "T" stop before Harvard, Central Square, gets you to a section of Massachusetts Avenue that spicy food lovers treasure as a trove of moderately priced Indian, Middle Eastern and Chinese restaurants. We have spent a good part of our life at these tables, and emerged well nourished, stimulated and enthused. Indian spice stores and Japanese groceries are in the neighborhood and, not far, in East Cambridge, Portuguese Restaurants (Casa Portugal is like a party), bakeries and grocery stores.

You could not ask for more of a culture shock than a jump-cut from the spicy food halls of Central Square to bucolic Lexington and Concord about fifteen minutes away. These historic towns could be reached by following Massachusetts Avenue, which becomes 2A, but the quick way to do it is Route 2, which will bring you—ten minutes after spicy *pakoras* on your plate!—into farm country and farmstands with seasonal produce.

Lexington and Concord proudly display pristine village greens, white clapboard churches and well preserved Colonial-style houses and farms. In Lexington, the first shots of the Revolutionary War were fired at dawn on April 19, 1775. Each year the town commemorates the event by reen-acting the battle on the town green, site of the Minuteman statues of Captain John Parker. Lexington's Museum of Our National Heritage runs imaginative shows on American history, Americana and decorative arts.

"The shot heard round the world" was fired at Concord's Old North Bridge. At Minuteman National Historic Park, you can watch an introductory film and then visit the battlefield.

To drive along Route 2A through Lexington and Concord is to motor through American history. The former homes of Louisa May Alcott, Nathaniel Hawthorne and Ralph Waldo Emerson, and the site of Henry David Thoreau's cabin on Walden Pond are literary landmarks, open to the public.

You may find yourself lingering in some wood west of Boston, wondering how like the wood you stand in was early Boston. There are fewer varieties of birds now, and we've depleted many species of plants, but the oaks still grow, and the maples, and the brook you follow will lead to a river and that river to Massachusetts Bay—where it all began.

BREADS

Faneuil Hall Marketplace, Boston

Pumpkin Bread

⅔ cup butter, softened

2½ cups sugar

4 Westminster Farm Eggs

2 cups cooked, mashed Marini Farm Pumpkin

¼ cup Hood Orange Juice

3⅓ cups all-purpose flour

1 tsp baking powder

2 tsp baking soda

1 tsp cinnamon

½ tsp nutmeg

⅔ cup chopped nuts, raisins or dates (optional)

- Preheat oven to 350 degrees.
- Thoroughly cream together butter and sugar.
- Beat in eggs; blend in pumpkin and orange juice.
- Sift dry ingredients and spices together; blend into mixture.
- Stir in nuts, raisins or dates, if desired.
- Spoon batter into 2 greased and lightly floured, 9″ x 5″ loaf pans.
- Bake 1 hour.
- Serves 18-20.

Pam's Zucchini Bread

3 Pine Hill Farm Eggs

1 cup vegetable oil

2 cups sugar

1 tsp vanilla

2½ cups peeled and grated Verrill Farm Zucchini

3 cups all-purpose flour

1 tbsp cinnamon

1½ tsp baking powder

1 tsp baking soda

1 tsp salt

1 cup chopped nuts

- Beat eggs until foamy.
- Add oil, sugar and vanilla; mix well.
- Stir in zucchini.
- Combine dry ingredients; mix until well blended.
- Fold in nuts.
- Pour into 2 greased and floured 9″ x 5″ loaf pans.
- Bake at 325 degrees 1 hour.
- Serves 18-20.

Banana Bread

½ cup butter, softened

½ cup Cumworth Farm Honey

2 eggs

½ cup yogurt

1 tsp vanilla

1½ cups New England Natural Bakers Honey Crunch or Maple Nut Granola

1 cup Green Friedman All-Purpose Flour

2 cups mashed banana

pinch of salt

1 tsp baking soda

1 tsp baking powder

- Cream butter and honey.
- Add eggs, yogurt and vanilla; mix well.
- Add granola and mix; set aside.
- Add flour, bananas, salt, baking soda and baking powder; mix well.
- Pour into 9″ x 5″ greased loaf pan.
- Bake at 350 degrees 1 hour, or until done.
- Serves 8-10.

Granola Carrot Bread

½ cup packed brown sugar

1½ cups New England Natural Bakers Granola

1½ cups Gray's Whole Wheat Flour

1½ cups grated Fowler Farm Carrots

½ cup vegetable oil

1 tbsp baking powder

1 tsp vanilla

½ tsp salt

2 eggs

½ cup milk

- Preheat oven to 350 degrees.
- Grease and flour 8½″ x 4½″ loaf pan.
- Combine all ingredients in bowl; stir until just mixed. Turn into loaf pan.
- Bake 55-60 minutes, or until cake tester inserted in center comes out clean.
- Cool 10 minutes in pan.
- Turn out onto rack to finish cooling.
- Serves 8-10.

Milk and Honey Bread

1 cup Brookside Farm Milk
⅔ cup honey
¼ cup butter
2 Hillside Farm Eggs
1½ cups all-purpose flour
1 cup Gray's Whole Wheat Flour
1 tbsp baking powder
1 tsp salt
½ cup toasted wheat germ
1 cup walnut halves

- Heat milk and honey until honey dissolves.
- Stir in butter.
- Cool; beat in eggs.
- Sift together dry ingredients.
- Add wheat germ.
- Gradually stir dry mixture into the liquid.
- Stir in walnuts; mix well.
- Bake in greased 9" x 5" loaf pan 1 hour at 350 degrees.
- Serves 8-10.

Cranberry Fruit Nut Bread

2 cups Green Friedman All-Purpose Flour
1 cup sugar
1¼ tsp baking powder
1 tsp salt
½ tsp baking soda
½ tsp nutmeg
½ tsp cinnamon
¼ cup shortening
1 Diemand Egg Farm Egg, beaten
1 tsp grated orange peel
¾ cup orange juice
1 cup chopped Paradise Meadows Cranberries
½ cup chopped nuts

- Sift together dry ingredients; cut in shortening.
- Combine peel, juice and egg.
- Add dry ingredients, mixing just until moistened.
- Fold in cranberries and nuts.
- Turn into greased 9" x 5" loaf pan.
- Bake at 350 degrees 1 hour.
- Cool, wrap and store overnight before slicing.
- Serves 8-10.

Cranberry Coffee Braid

1 loaf frozen bread dough

1 (12 oz) pkg Ocean Spray
Cran-Fruit™ Sauce

½ cup chopped walnuts

1 tsp cinnamon

1 cup powdered sugar

2 tbsp water

- Preheat oven to 375 degrees.
- Thaw dough according to pkg directions. Drain cranberry fruit sauce.
- Roll out dough on lightly floured surface, into 11" x 15" rectangle, ¼" thick.
- In small mixing bowl, combine cranberry fruit sauce, nuts and cinnamon; spread lengthwise down center of dough in 3"-4" wide strip.
- With knife, make 1" wide slices in dough to within ½" of filling.
- Fold dough strips alternately across center of cake, forming a braid.
- Let rise in warm place for 30 minutes.
- Bake braid 30 minutes, or until golden brown; cool.
- Combine powdered sugar and water; drizzle glaze on braid.
- Best if served same day.
- Serves 8-10.

Raisin Bran Muffins

1¼ cups Super Raisin Bran

1¼ cups Gray's Whole Wheat Flour

2 tsp baking powder

2 eggs

¼ cup vegetable oil

¼ cup New Morning
Blackstrap Molasses

¼ honey

- Preheat oven to 350 degrees.
- Line muffin tins with paper baking cups or grease with margarine for best results.
- Combine raisin bran, flour and baking powder.
- Blend all liquid ingredients and mix thoroughly with dry ingredients.
- Fill muffin cups ⅔ full and bake 20-30 minutes.
- Makes 1 doz.

Blueberry Coffeecake

4 cups Green Friedman
All-Purpose Flour

1½ cups sugar

1 tbsp plus 2 tsp baking powder

1½ tsp salt

½ cup shortening

1½ cup Brookside Farm Milk

2 eggs

4 cups fresh Patt's Blueberries

Topping:

1 cup sugar

⅔ cup Green Friedman
All-Purpose Flour

1 tsp cinnamon

½ cup butter, softened

Glaze:

2 cups powdered sugar

¼ cup butter

1 tsp Charles H. Baldwin &
Sons Vanilla

⅓-½ cup water

- Beat together all ingredients, except blueberries, for ½ minute.
- Stir in blueberries.
- Fill 2 cake pans half way.
- Mix together all topping ingredients; sprinkle on top of mixtures in cake pans.
- Bake 45-50 minutes at 375 degrees.
- Cool slightly before glazing.
- Mix together all glaze ingredients, adding water carefully, until desired spreading consistency.
- Drizzle glaze on coffeecakes.
- Serves 12-16.

Oat Bran Muffins

2 cups New Morning Organic Oat
Bran Cereal
2 tsp baking powder
½ cup honey or molasses
1 cup Hood Silouet Skim Milk
2 tbsp vegetable oil

- Preheat oven to 425 degrees.
- Line muffin cups with paper baking cups, or brush bottoms with vegetable oil.
- Combine dry ingredients.
- Add honey or molasses, milk and oil; mixing just until dry ingredients are moistened.
- Fill muffin cups ⅔ full and bake 15-17 minutes.
- Makes 1 doz.

Variations:
Add to batter any of the following:

- ¼ cup raisins and ¼ cup nuts.
- 1 medium banana, mashed, and ¼ cup nuts.
- ½ cup fresh or frozen blueberries.
- ½ cup chopped apples, ¼ cup nuts and 1 tsp cinnamon.

Oyster Stuffing for Turkey

2 cups shucked oysters, drained
2 cups crumbled Bent's Water Crackers
1 cup Hood Light Cream
4 tbsp melted butter
salt and pepper

- Place oysters and cracker crumbs in large bowl.
- Pour in cream and butter, season with salt and pepper. Mix well.
- Let stand 1 hour to allow flavors to blend.
- Makes 5 cups.

Jordan Marsh Blueberry Muffins

½ cup butter
1 cup sugar
2 Otis Eggs
2 cups all-purpose flour
4 tsp baking powder
⅔ cups Gibson Village Farm Dairy Milk
1¼ cup Tougas Farm Blueberries
sugar to garnish

- Cream butter and sugar, then add eggs, flour, baking powder and milk.
- Dredge berries in additional flour before adding to wet mixture to prevent sticking.
- Bake at 350 degrees 30 minutes.
- Remove from oven and sprinkle a little sugar on muffin tops.
- Makes 1 doz.

Cheese Muffinettes

1¾ cups Green Friedman All-Purpose Flour
1 tbsp baking powder
¼ tsp salt
2 tbsp poppy seeds
⅔ cup finely shredded Cheddar cheese
1 Whip-O-Will Farm Egg, beaten
¾ cup milk
¼ cup Welch's White Grape Juice
3 tbsp melted butter

- Preheat oven to 400 degrees.
- In large mixing bowl, combine flour, baking powder, salt, poppy seeds and cheese.
- Combine all liquid ingredients in large measuring cup; mix to blend.
- Combine the liquid and dry ingredients together.
- Fill greased muffin cups ¾ full and bake 20-25 minutes.
- Makes 1 doz.

CAPE COD

Loving a person and loving a place aren't really so different. The lift and surge and sudden happiness are much the same. And the feelings on seeing them—landscape or lover—after an absence are akin.

When I pilot my auto, "Ruby," across the sturdy, graceful Sagamore Bridge at the northern end of the Cape Cod Canal, I am returning to a beloved place. The drive across the bridge feels like crossing a room, climbing a stair, or opening the door knowing that a loved one waits. The trip is short—less than a minute across the sparkling canal—but charged with anticipation.

To reach the sandy shore of Cape Cod is to leave the leaden concerns of everyday—earning a living, keeping up with the news, arresting the forces of entropy in one's domicile—to abide for a while in a place of unique comfort. Where much is beautiful, interesting and pleasing.

The Cape, that peninsula turned island by the construction of the seventeen-mile canal in the early part of the twentieth century, has been enchanting me for over twenty years. And though it and I have changed, it has never lost its allure.

There is, most of all, the topography and geography, the fortunate accident of its glacial birth over 10,000 years ago. As it's surrounded by water, the Cape's temperatures are always moderated—warmer in winter and cooler in summer, especially at night when the winds pick up and there are no dark red Bostonian buildings to hold the heat.

The topography and varied landscape are sufficiently diverse to explore for a lifetime. The upper, western part of the Cape is flat and green, good terrain for farming and raising trout in enormous artificial pools, which is what the Commonwealth of Massachusetts does, then moves the speckled, darting critters to local rivers and brooks.

Mashpee has dense woods where rhododendron, mountain laurel and wild azalea grow, often on the edge of azure ponds where families of mallards abide. In Harwich, the lowlands allow for flooding and the garnet haze of ripening cranberries in autumn.

In Chatham, on the "elbow" of Cape Cod in the southeast, the gardens are unimaginably lush because of the town's legendary fog. Every lawn looks like a golf course, the beech trees grow to preternatural magnitude and the salt spray roses spill over arbors and picket fences.

Head north to the outer Cape and you'll find the lush green marshes of South Wellfleet, where the Massachusetts Audubon Society has its Wellfleet Bay Wildlife Sanctuary.

The winding roads, hummocks and hills of Truro will make you feel you're in Scotland or Cornwall. Truro, in Cornish, means "place of the hill."

The varied habitats of the Cape Cod National Seashore, 27,000-acres sprawling across Eastham, Wellfleet, Truro and Provincetown, dominating the Outer Cape, range from the Atlantic White Cedar Swamp to freshwater ponds to the majestic dune-swept tip of Provincetown.

So, perhaps you can imagine why Cape Cod makes us feel on safari, piloting our (alas, imaginary) Land Rover from terrain to terrain. We will never tire of the variety of beaches. The outline of sundry natural harbors. The scores of saltwater, fresh water and brackish ponds, each a little world.

Please examine a map of Cape Cod to appreciate why Cape beaches (and everything associated with them—birds, plants, human visitors) are diverse. Beaches on the Upper Cape on Cape Cod Bay are safe, charming, beguiling because of the relative calm of the bay waters. They're called "bay beaches."

The same character holds for beaches on the southern length of the Cape, those on Vineyard Sound or Nantucket Sound. This shore—stretching from the village of Woods Hole in Falmouth to the town of Chatham—is called the "sound side" of the Cape.

As soon as you reach the Outer Cape—that dramatic eastern Atlantic shore, the character of the wind and water and the sculpture of the sand change.

In Chatham, there are waves and a powerful surf that's reshaped the beach in recent years, creating an unwelcome inlet, a good deal of erosion and placing dozens of houses in jeopardy. The magnificent Atlantic, it must be remembered, goes its way, not ours.

By the time you reach Nauset Beach in Orleans, the long north-south barrier beach has become expansive, endless seeming, with a profusion of grasses, dusty miller and twirling purple beach pea, and the waves are sufficiently grand that surfers are in sight. Continue north to Provincetown and the drama escalates. Majestic dunes rise up, the waves mount, curve, then crash against the beach. At sunset a vivid orange fireball descends.

Similar ranges of variation exist both in local dress and cuisine. Town by town, there are discrete local customs, habits and habitats; different items appear on menus and different haberdashery is on parade.

While faded jeans, a decent sweatshirt and comfortable shoes are seen from Woods Hole to Wellfleet, and ambrosial fried clams are available most anywhere, there are differences.

Woods Hole is a kind of Cantabrigian Cape Cod, where dress is free form and hip. Provincetown is the artsy, bohemian center of Cape Cod and *outre-chic* reigns. Except, of course, if you're a fisherman, in which case yellow oilskins reign.

In Chatham, lots of people are playing golf and women are wearing pearls, even with Bermuda shorts. They're feasting on strawberry shortcake in Chatham—made with real whipped cream and local berries—while in P-town it's sorbet with tuile cookies, or the new food phase, "comfort food," which might feature a luscious devil's food cake, blueberry pie with slivers of crystallized ginger, or golly gee, strawberry shortcake with cream on top....

Come to think of it, maybe Chatham and P-town aren't so far apart these days. Shared and sharing food may be the answer to the quest for world peace.

Perhaps we can justify our own keen interest in food this way. It doesn't *really* have to do with pleasure, but with geopolitical unity. With anthropology. Meteorology. Beyond all justification, we do associate different places and seasons on Cape Cod with different foods.

Summer free-associates at once with the irresistible aroma of deep fried clams eaten outdoors at Nauset Beach. We know just the right beach-shack in East Orleans—you can't miss it—and would walk more than a mile for their unvarnished, unequaled presentation: succulent, crisp clam-bodies, served in a paper tray with lemon slices, tartar sauce, cole slaw. The little "wings" of the clam are like the ultimate in thin, crisp, onion rings and the meat of the clam like a delicately sauteed oyster.

Fried clams can only lead to visions of clam chowder and we've sampled it in many seasons and many moods on Cape Cod. (It is definitely an anti-depressant.) We like it best in odd places in Provincetown, where they might throw in a little *linguica*—spicy Portuguese sausage—for flavor. We prefer eating it in autumn and winter, but we must call your attention to a particular form of chowder madness: WCOD, a Cape Cod radio station, stages an annual Chowder Festival at the Cape Cod Melody Tent in Hyannis. The soup-in is usually in June and features samples from dozens of Cape Cod restaurants.

Choose your favorite and you'll be set for summer. After all, what could make a better supper-in-a-bowl than aromatic chowder with oyster-ettes? (Demand oysterettes. Accept no substitutes. Ordinary crackers do not float, bob, or crunch.)

We cannot deny that summer often leads us to one of the Cape's many homemade ice cream emporia. As we have already verged far from the Pritikin diet with our fried clams repast—and shared our neighbor's onion rings—we may as well forget it, right?

Cape Cod ice cream begins with fresh cream and often features local berries, something summery and all-American or even something a little exotic. As we're feasting at Nauset Beach, we'd locate an ice cream shop on nearby Main Street where we'd select Grapenut, Black Raspberry with Chocolate Chips, or Ginger. In the first case, the rich vanilla ice cream base would be interrupted by tiny, chewy molasses flavored pellets. In the second, the tart creamy raspberry flavor would have slivers of dark chocolate, a concept that derives from the French practice of serving dense chocolate desserts with raspberry coulis. Or that third option, ginger would be pale apricot in color with shavings of crystallized ginger.

If we had a cottage on the Cape in summer, we'd be on the prowl for local corn, local tomatoes and homemade jams. Beach plum jelly—made from vitamin-C-intensive rosehips—is sold at many shops in Cape Cod. But no shop is as compelling as that in a 200-year old house in East Sandwich. Imagine a nature and ecology center *cum* jam kitchen and shop, and you've sort of got it.

It is the Green Briar Nature Center and Jam Kitchen, operated by the nonprofit Thornton Burgess Society. Burgess, who was born in Sandwich, is the naturalist and children's author known for his Peter Rabbit tales. He roamed the woods and ponds of Green Briar, which inspired the literary world he created. Meanwhile, back at the Jam Kitchen—where classes in jam making are taught, not to mention natu-ral history courses—the most inspired jams, jellies and fruit sauces are available. Blueberries with kirsch. Rhubarb with ginger. Plums with rum.

Autumn is radiantly, indelibly associated with cranberries, which grow wild in wet meadows and bogs all over Cape Cod, especially in the Province Lands of Provincetown, Sandy Neck in Sandwich and Monomoy Island off Chatham. You can walk a trail through a cranberry bog off North Pamet Road in Truro, part of the National Seashore's trail system. In Harwich, cultivated cranberries are a leading commercial crop. In September the town presents a two-week Cranberry Festival with parade, fireworks, arts and crafts shows and the gala Cranberry Ball.

Fall, of course, is when the noble, tart little berry is harvested. And on Cape Cod, it's used for a lot more than cranberry sauce. You'll find it in breads, cakes, muffins, dressings and delectable bread puddings. Tonier restaurants will use it in piquant sauces served with pheasant and duck, cooked with game, or even trout. You'll find cranberry pies and cobblers and excellent tarts. On slim-down days, we spice up on cottage cheese with a side of cranberry relish.

There are small apple orchards on Cape Cod and in autumn you'll find apples, the new crop of winter squash and cranberries at farm stands. These three fruits (we believe squash is botanically a fruit) lend themselves to many tasty, autumnal creations. Try putting cranberries in your apple pie, making a casserole of apples, butternut squash, cranberries and toasted walnuts.

Celebrating Thanksgiving in New England is always special, and a festive dinner on the Cape at this time of year is unforgettable. The leaves of the Cape's majestic oaks and maples are turning, the air is cool with a tang and you'll want to take long walks on the beach and down country lanes. It's a time to visit one of the Cape's bed and breakfast places, or to enjoy the leisurely lobster dinner you might have missed in summer.

Great time, too, to visit the galleries in Wellfleet and Provincetown, to motor from port to port on the "sound side," to idle at Scargo Pottery in Dennis, where pots are shaped before your eyes and the vivid ceramics are displayed in a semi-outdoor gallery open to pine woods and bird song.

A few historic mills still grind corn on Cape Cod, notably Baxter Grist Mill in West Yarmouth, built almost three hundred years ago, and Thomas Dexter's Grist Mill in Sandwich, in its striking site on Shawme Pond. Buy this good stuff and make up a mess of cornbread or johnny cake. It has lots of crunch and B-vitamins and is a complementary protein if eaten with milk or cheese.

Corn and cornmeal are meaningful on Cape Cod. The ancestors of America owed their lives to it. At one of the most popular beaches on Cape Cod, Corn Hill in Truro, Pilgrim leader Miles Standish discovered a cache of Indian corn. He took it, or borrowed it, or stole it, depending on your point of view. He and sixteen Pilgrims planted it. The cache of corn became their first crop.

Winter Cape culinary associations run to oyster stew and turkeys and small birds stuffed with cornbread and cranberries. It's a time for adding cream to the chowder and for Indian pudding, a divine stick-to-the-ribs dessert of cornmeal, molasses, eggs and milk, served with vanilla ice cream or a dollop of softly whipped cream.

When the wind really blows in winter, take yourself to Provincetown and seek out some hearty Portuguese stews and soups, often salty and smoky with the flavor of *linguica*, a sausage that changes mundane to sassy. Kale soup looks a little Christmasy, with its dark green leaves and bits of tomato. Or maybe it's just the influence of the Abstract Expressionists who painted in Provincetown. Maybe they're on our minds as we study our soup.

In spring, we rush the season by packing up a big beach picnic and consume our chowder-in-thermos or sandwiches with Cape Cod potato chips, a delectable local product that contains no added salt. We motor by small farm stands that showcase the new crop of dewey sweet peas, tender leaf lettuce, pencil-slim asparagus and ruby-colored rhubarb.

But how can this diversity exist on such a small site, you ask. Especially if said site is not exactly in the midst of the South Pacific. From downtown Boston—traffic on Route 3 cooperating—it's just an hour to the Sagamore Bridge. (There are two bridges that cross the canal. If you're coming from Boston, you take the Sagamore. From Buzzard's Bay and points south, the Bourne.) From the canal, it's about an hour to Orleans, another forty minutes to Provincetown.

Well, firstly, Cape Cod is in New England, where people are individualistic, if not ornery. And the Bill of Rights is talked about as though it were breaking news.

Secondly, Cape Cod is very old. People have been living here and working out their jurisdictions, preferences and peculiarities for generations. Many Native Americans, mainly Mashpee Wampanoags, still live on Cape Cod, and hold their pow-wows in Mashpee, reminding visitors that the seventeenth century colonials were new Americans — immigrants.

And thirdly, there are fifteen towns and scores of villages, hamlets and enclaves in this glorious kingdom of sand, cranberries, oysters and cod. Each town has its own post office, bakery, general (or convenience) store, watering hole, secret swimming hole and politics.

And there are summer people, year-round people, native people (year-round *born* Cape Codders) and retired people. And people who come to buy, to drive, to see sights and make noise. And people who come to be quiet, be absorbed, to study the patterns of waves.

So, what exactly is this place that Patti Page sang of? Cape Cod, named for its local crop, is a big sand spit, stretching seventy miles into the Atlantic Ocean. It is also the birthplace of the concept of America. On November 11, 1620, the Pilgrims first dropped anchor in Provincetown. They remained anchored for six cold, hopeful weeks.

Parties of Pilgrim men explored the area and found the place not exactly what they were looking for. The land was sandy, the waters hard to navigate.

The Pilgrim fathers decided to sail south for richer soil and safer harbors and made their first colony at Plymouth (Plimoth, actually) on Massachusetts' south shore. But before they left the waters of Cape Cod, they signed the Mayflower Compact, a historic commitment to self-government.

Three Mayflower passengers died during the weeks the Pilgrims were anchored. They are buried in Eastham on the Outer Cape. A child, Peregrine White, was born, the first child of European settlers born in New England.

As more settlers came to Plymouth, various groups emigrated to Cape Cod, settling first in Sandwich, Barnstable, Yarmouth and Eastham, where salt hay provided fodder for cattle. Schools and churches were built.

The early settlers farmed, fished, traded and built boats. All these pursuits remain. Tourism has taken over as the major business of Cape Cod, but Wellfleet oysters still show up in Carmel, California—probably with a bit of pimento or basil, or some such frivolous garnish—and the catch of Chatham's stalwart fishermen is being served in Manhattan restaurants within a day of their life in the sea.

In shape, Cape Cod resembles an upturned arm pointing north toward Provincetown. Its towns, villages and ports are served by three main roads that converge at Orleans on the Outer Cape.

The roads are fine, but the orientation is a little weird. Finding your way on Cape Cod is at first a little confusing. South Chatham is west of West Chatham. North Harwich is west of East Harwich. That kind of thing. And too many ponds are called Herring Pond. Same thing with the rivers.

King's Highway is Route 6A, though during the late 1930s its name was changed to Grand Army of the Republic Highway. Innkeepers sometimes refer to the road as the Cranberry Highway, but you don't see that appellation on signs, which doesn't help much when you're trying to find your inn. What you need to know is that if you're on a road and you see signs that proclaim G.A.R. Highway, you're on Route 6A. Or some town's Main Street.

The Upper Cape is the chunk from the canal to the "elbow." The Lower Cape goes from Dennis up to Provincetown (though you would never say "up" on the Cape; we'll explain). Except that nobody who lives on Cape Cod ever uses the term Lower Cape; it's known as the more descriptive Outer Cape—the upward forearm that faces outward on the Atlantic.

Regardless of where you are or where you're headed, "down-Cape" means in the direction of Provincetown and "up-Cape" means toward the canal. Jingoistic Bostonians sometimes resent the term "up-Cape" because you have to go down to drive from Boston, which is, after all the Hub. They insist on saying that "they're going down Cape." Which may, to them, mean Provincetown, but it certainly won't to a Cape Codder.

Oh, yes. Some people will also use the term "mid-Cape." It means the Barnstable, Yarmouth, Dennis-area. The best thing to do, as Kerouac knew, was to forget the terms and get on the road.

The road. There are three biggies, each of different character. Route 6A on the north side, the bay side of Cape Cod, follows the shore from Sandwich to Orleans. You can't really see the shore, but this is a grand old road, the Main Street of several towns. It winds a lot in places and takes you over ponds here and there. You'll pass inns and B&Bs, antique shops and barns, lots of classy houses and a fair share of oddities and quiddities.

When you get to Parnassus Book Store in Yarmouth, stop. It sure doesn't look like Waldenbooks. The window display is mainly dust overlaying zillions of books. Inside are zillions more, mainly second-hand. You will find everything from a spiral bound 1953 cookbook with photographs of casseroles direct from the Donna Reed show to a flawless copy of a wine encyclopedia to a Russian novel (in Russian) in crumbling paperback to a handsome vintage set of Churchill's histories.

But we digress. Which is what you cannot do if you choose Route 6. You may wish to if you're on a schedule. Route 6 is the Mid-Cape Highway. It starts at the Sagamore Bridge and continues without diversion or distraction to the Eastham-Orleans Rotary. It then becomes the only road on the Outer Cape and leads from Orleans to Provincetown. If you take 6A from the Sagamore, you'll still have to hit Route 6 to head north. Route 6 turns into your basic, all American trashy road in places north of Orleans, but it also leads to the National Seashore Headquarters in North Eastham and to the very tip of Provincetown.

Route 28 starts at Bourne just over the Bourne bridge, the southern bridge over the canal, and heads to Falmouth on the "sound side." It then heads east to Chatham and jogs north to end at the Orleans rotary. (Just before you get to the rotary, check out a series of galleries in Orleans on Route 28. Route 28 has the digression possibilities of Route 6A.)

Route 28 is not bucolic. It passes through many pretty Cape towns, but also through a lot of *stuff* on the outskirts—shops, fast food restaurants and motel lodgings. Learn to love it. This is America. And keep a map in your lap so you can see how close you are to the southern shore.

Space will not allow us to convey socio-politico-culinary sketches of all fifteen of Cape Cod's towns, not to mention villages such as Yarmouthport in Yarmouth, or Cataumet in Bourne, between Red Brook Harbor and Squeteague Harbor (yes, squeteague is an Indian word, a local fish Native Americans used to make glue.) But we'll try to give you a sense of the spread, the glorious variety of these towns.

For first time visitors, there's a rush of impressions.

Winding Route 6A, the old road that follows the line of Cape Cod Bay—connecting Sandwich, Barnstable, Yarmouth, Dennis, Brewster— is a delight for antique fanciers and architecture buffs. Nature trails off the beaten path. The smell of bayberry brushing your shirt, sassafras crushed underfoot.

Shipshape Woods Hole with its jaunty harborside cafes and gleaming white ferries making their way to Martha's Vineyard and Nantucket.

The intricate inlets and twinkling harbors along Nantucket Sound, a chain of small town main streets and ports, from Falmouth to Cotuit and Osterville; Hyannis Port, South Yarmouth, Dennis Port, Harwich Port. The fragrance of steamed mussels and clams.

The extravagant, genteel quality of Chatham, with its grand hotel on the sea and impeccably kept summer properties with deep manicured lawns. Its lighthouse, monument and Coast Guard station. Simple pleasures: fudge, ice cream, salt water taffy.

The almost mythical lure of the Outer Cape—Chatham, Orleans,

Eastham, Wellfleet and small, mysterious Truro, an enclave of woods, heaths, moors, hills, azalea swamps and the majestic vantage of the Atlantic. Finding the beach you hoped you would—with dunes, the sweep of surf and hummocks of sea lavender. A farm stand with a nine-year-old girl selling tiny, frosted wild blueberries.

Provincetown with its rich literary history. So this is where Eugene O'Neill struggled and wrote. Galleries, cinema, cafes, a lively shopping scene. A majestic beach, the jewel in the National Seashore's crown. Spicy, smoky kale soup. Portuguese bakeries with "portuguese toast"—like French toast, but made with fluffier, eggier, Portuguese bread.

Most of all, first time visitors remember the marvels of the Cape Cod National Seashore, which stretches from Nauset Light Beach in Eastham to the Provincetown's Race Point. The specifics run to six protected beaches, two spacious visitor centers, bicycle trails through meadows, dunes, around kettle ponds and a variety of self-guiding nature trails through, around and over marshes, bogs, beaches, dunes, ponds and of course the Atlantic.

Stay a few weeks and the melange of impressions starts to sort and cohere. Study your map. Observe the terrain and your fellow citizens. Read about Cape Cod. Hang out.

Sandwich, the oldest town on Cape Cod, established 1637, has a handsome town center with grand colonial and Greek Revival homes and a church with a Christopher Wren-inspired steeple. Its many family attractions include the Thornton W. Burgess Museum, tribute to the children's author, and Green Briar Nature Center, which offers nature walks and talks for children.

The Sandwich Glass Museum has wonderfully displayed pressed, patterned and colored glass made at the internationally known Sandwich glass factory founded in 1825. Heritage Plantation, a seventy-five acre showplace farm turned arboretum and museum, has hundreds of varieties of rhododendrons and specimen trees and a superb collection of Americana—a vintage carousel in working order, antique cars, wood and ceramic folk art and 150 Currier & Ives prints.

Barnstable, in the mid-Cape area, is an old whaling town, now an enclave of gracious homes on a sheltered harbor, a celebrated departure point for sport fishermen. There are fine B&Bs in this area, superb biking terrain and the Donald G. Trayser Memorial Museum in the 1856 Customs House conveying Barnstable's maritime legacy.

"It is better that this country set sail than lie still in the harbor," says the inscription on the John F. Kennedy memorial in Hyannis, where the former president sailed and where the family compound is still located at Hyannis Port. Hyannis is the hub of the Cape, with its largest airport, seasonal ferry service to Martha's Vineyard and Nantucket and fishing and scenic excursions.

If you like your beaches warm and cozy, those of the mid-Cape towns of Hyannis, Yarmouth and Dennis are for you. The mid-Cape is family terrain—charming oceanfront restaurants, colorful summer theater, fishing charters and dolphin shows.

Falmouth has a classic village green and a profusion of nineteenth century houses, many with salt spray roses tumbling over trellises and gates. Woods Hole, the village at the southern tip of Falmouth, has a laid-back, academic air. (Imagine aspects of Cambridge transported to a fishing village.) It's the site of several world class scientific organizations, including the Woods Hole Oceanographic Institute.

Scientists need to think, eat, drink coffee and look out the window while doing so. There is nothing better to watch than the coming and going of boats, especially if there is a drawbridge. Therefore, Woods Hole boasts delightful informal seafood cafes—one devoted to natural foods is especially good—where a patron may bring a book and read while nursing mugs of strong coffee or heavy bowls of chowder.

The local bookstore stocks erudite scientific and nautical periodicals cheek-by-jowl with best-sellers and paperback classics. In Woods Hole, you read, you walk, you eat seafood.

In summer the Woods Hole Aquarium is open to the public. And in all seasons, it's *de rigueur* to take a turn in St. Margaret's Garden on Millfield Street with its luminous view of the harbor and backdrop of the town.

Ashumet Holly Reservation in nearby East Falmouth is open all year. It's best in winter when newly fallen snow makes a perfect foil for the glossy holly leaves and bright red berries.

Chatham has aristocratic leanings, a patrician air, with beautifully kept old houses, deep lawns, golf courses, a grand hotel and inns on the sea. The tidy, picturesque beaches are easy to find, the handsome library is prominently situated on Main Street and the Railroad Museum in its original Victorian depot is, of course, on Depot Street.

Chatham boasts some of the most magnificent trees on Cape Cod— some European beeches are the size of a house!—and the gardens are exemplary, a tribute to the beneficial effects of fog. In summer, spirited concerts are conducted at the town bandstand, in July a Strawberry Festival is held on the verdant grounds of a church and the Annual Festival of the Arts each August is a time for savoring art outdoors. Chatham Light, the town's splendid signature lighthouse, attracts visitors at all times of year, as does the product of its fishing fleet. Don't leave this town without a visit to the fisherman's coop. You'll find lobster, scallops, cod, bluefish, mackerel, flounder and sometimes tuna. It doesn't get fresher than this.

Wellfleet, a wonderfully intricate town of artists, poets and fisherfolk, is quirkier, less obvious than many Cape towns. You must explore various byways to find its treasures—the shining harbor with Indian Neck and Mayo Beach; Newcomb Hollow, Cahoon Hollow, White Crest and LeCount Hollow beaches off Ocean View Drive in South Wellfleet and the secret, secluded freshwater ponds in pine woods off Ocean View Drive. Visit Chequesset Neck for extraordinary sunsets.

Wellfleet's shellfish beds and fishing grounds yield the celebrated Wellfleet oyster, along with tiny, delicate bay scallops, *quahogs* (a big clam, pronounced koHOG), mussels, razor clams, blue crabs and sea clams. Look for these and other seafood in local restaurants.

Harbor restaurants in town serve oysters, chowders, clam cakes, lobster-in-the-rough and there are also elegant, "linen tablecloth restaurants." A day at the beach, a shower at your inn, slipping on fresh clothes and communing with loved ones over Wellfleet oysters and white wine is definitely a reason to carry on.

The next morning is for walking along Wellfleet's Main Street, checking on general stores, funky restaurants, the library and cultural activities and events. The Wellfleet Historical Society, once a village shop, overflows with intriguing documentation of the town's long life—tales of whaling, sailing, oystering, plus saltworks and railroads.

The energy level in Provincetown is high. This tightly knit village has long been an artists' colony and is surrounded by land of spectacular beauty. In summer, Commercial Street—the main street of rambling old houses, inns, scores of restaurants, cafes, bistros, boutiques, galleries, jewelry and leather stores—is hip, colorful and occasionally outrageous. In autumn and winter it reverts to its introspective, off-season self, a fishing village where painters, poets, playwrights and writers are hard at work.

Because of the diversity of Cape Cod, you can suit yourself, zipping from end to end or anywhere in between along Route 6. Or, you can focus on particular interests.

Naturalists will want to spend a lot of time at the National Seashore, Massachusetts Audubon's Wellfleet Bay Wildlife Sanctuary and at the National Wildlife Refuge at Monomoy Island off Chatham. The Cape Cod Museum of Natural History in Brewster has rewarding trails that lead through examples of Cape Cod flora and fauna. Navigators will quickly identify coastal waters and preferred ports. Fisherfolk have a lot of choices, but should make a point of visiting Rock Harbor in Orleans, where over a dozen sport fishing charters tie-up. History buffs can choose among scores of local historical societies, house museums and well stocked libraries. Art lovers will find most to attract them in Wellfleet and Provincetown.

Those who like the focus of specific events will enjoy the Barnstable Country Fair in Falmouth in July and the jubilant Scallop Festivals in Chatham and Bourne in October.

Cape Cod cognoscenti know that autumn is actually the most beautiful time, though there will always be madcap partisans of summer. In autumn you can walk for miles and miles along the outer beaches, the bright blue Atlantic on one side, the undulating dunes and tangle of tousled beach pea on the other, with hardly a soul in sight.

The problem, at the end, is returning over that symbolic bridge. Crossing the canal. It feels terribly wrong to be going the other way! Before you know it, the wind and the good Cape air are gone, along with the whitecaps and sound of the sea.

For those who've really succumbed to Cape Cod, those with "sand in their shoes," many moments of many days and nights will be devoted to thinking about Cape Cod. What it felt like. Why. And how to get back again. It is very like a love affair.

SOUPS

Quaint Cape Cod

Corn Chowder

⅓ cup cubed salt pork

½ cup peeled, chopped Wilson Farm Onion

¼ cup chopped Wilson Farm Green Pepper

1½ cups hot water

1½ cups peeled, cubed potatoes

3 cups fresh Wilson Farm Corn Kernels

½ tsp salt

⅛ tsp pepper

2 cups West Lynn Creamery Milk

1 cup West Lynn Creamery Light Cream

- Cook salt pork in 4 qt pot until crisp.
- Add onion and pepper; cook until soft.
- Remove salt pork and vegetables from pan with slotted spoon; drain fat from pan.
- Return salt pork and vegetables to pan and add hot water, potatoes, corn, salt and pepper.
- Bring mixture to simmer; cook, covered, 10-15 minutes, or until potatoes are tender.
- Add milk, cream and additional seasoning, if necessary.
- Heat chowder; do not boil.
- When chowder is very hot, remove from heat; let sit 30 minutes to improve flavor.
- Reheat and serve.
- Serves 8.

Spinach Soup

1½ lbs fresh spinach leaves

3 cups water

2½ tbsp East India Instant India Curry Paste

1 tbsp Hood Whipping Cream or Sour Cream

1 cup milk (optional)

grated Parmesan cheese

freshly ground pepper

- Wash spinach thoroughly so that no sand remains. Place spinach in saucepan; add water. Bring to boil.
- Turn off heat; let cool 10 minutes.
- Puree boiled spinach in blender.
- Add curry paste to puree; reheat to serving temperature.
- Turn off heat; add whipping or sour cream and milk, if necessary.
- Sprinkle on cheese, add pepper to taste and serve hot.
- Serves 4.

Zucchini and Cheddar Cheese Soup

2½ cups chicken broth, divided

¼ cup chopped Wilson Farm Onion

⅓ cup chopped Wilson Farm Celery

5 cups unpeeled, sliced Wilson Farm Zucchini

½ tsp salt

⅛ tsp pepper

2 tbsp butter

2 tbsp all-purpose flour

½ cup Cooper's Hilltop Farm Light Cream

1 cup lightly packed, grated medium sharp Cheddar cheese

- Place 2 cups broth, onion, celery, zucchini, salt and pepper in 4 qt saucepan.
- Cover, bring to boil; lower heat and simmer, covered 20-25 minutes, or until soft.
- Puree mixture in small batches in blender or food processor; set aside.
- To make cheese sauce, melt butter in 2 qt saucepan and add flour; cook, stirring, 1 minute.
- Remove from heat and stir in remaining broth and cream.
- Return to heat and cook, stirring, until mixture thickens and begins to boil.
- Remove from heat; stir in cheese. When cheese melts, stir sauce into pureed vegetables.
- Add more salt and pepper to taste.
- Heat gently; do not boil.
- Add more cream if soup is too thick.
- Serves 6-8.

Pesto Tortellini Soup

1 tbsp olive oil

1 small onion, finely chopped

2-3 green onions, thinly sliced

1 stalk celery, diced

1 carrot, julienned

6-8 cups chicken broth

1 (9 oz) pkg Trio's Three Cheese Tortellini

1 (6 oz) jar Trio's Pesto Sauce

2 tbsp grated Parmesan cheese

- In 3 qt stock pot, heat olive oil and cook onion until golden.
- Add green onions, celery, carrot and chicken broth.
- Bring to simmer and add tortellini.
- Cook according to pkg directions.
- Turn off heat and add 1 tbsp pesto sauce to pot.
- Serve immediately, putting an extra dollop of pesto in each bowl and sprinkling with cheese.
- Serves 4-6.

Spanish Gazpacho

3 Bolton Orchards Tomatoes, cored and coarsely chopped

1½ cups peeled and coarsely chopped cucumber

1 green pepper, cored, seeded and chopped

1 clove garlic, sliced

½ cup water

5 tbsp olive oil

¼ cup Bear Meadow Farm Basil Vinegar

salt

2 slices untrimmed Montilios Bread, cubed

- Combine all ingredients in blender.
- Blend at high speed until well mixed.
- Place large sieve inside mixing bowl.
- Pour gazpacho into sieve, then press and stir with wooden spoon to extract as much juice as possible. Discard solids.
- Add more salt or vinegar if desired. Chill thoroughly.
- Serves 4-6.

Minted Summer Squash Soup

1 cup Hood Half & Half

½ cup fresh packed mint leaves

¼ cup butter

¾ cup sliced green onions

½ cup shredded Fowler Farm Carrot

1 clove garlic, minced

5 cups sliced mixed Spence Farm Summer Squash (pattypan, yellow and zucchini)

3 cups condensed chicken broth

salt and pepper

- Place cream and mint in blender container; cover.
- Puree until smooth; set aside.
- Melt butter in large saucepan.
- Saute onions, carrot and garlic until tender, about 5 minutes.
- Add squash and broth.
- Heat to boiling. Simmer, covered, 10-12 minutes, or until squash is tender.
- Place ⅓ squash mixture in blender container; cover. Puree until smooth.
- Repeat with remaining squash mixture.
- Return puree to saucepan.
- Season to taste with salt and pepper.
- Heat thoroughly, but do not boil.
- Stir in reserved cream mixture.
- Serve immediately.
- Serves 4-6.

Fresh Tomato Soup

2 tbsp butter

¼ cup minced Hibbard Farm Onion

2 cloves garlic, minced

3½ cups fresh tomato puree

2 (13.75 oz) cans chicken broth

1 cup Welch's White Grape Juice

¼ cup freshly minced parsley

½ cup freshly minced basil

basil and cooked shrimp to garnish

- In large stock pot or saucepan, heat butter over medium heat to melt.
- Add onion and garlic, saute until soft.
- Add tomato puree, broth, white grape juice and herbs; mix well.
- Bring mixture to boil; reduce heat and simmer 45 minutes.
- Chill or serve hot.
- Garnish each serving with fresh basil and shrimp.
- Serves 4-6.

Iced Spinach Soup

½ cup butter

¼ cup diced onion

¼ cup all-purpose flour

1 tsp salt

½ tsp dry mustard

¼ tsp nutmeg

1¼ cups chicken broth

½ cup shredded Fowler Farm Carrots

1½ cups cooked Fowler Farm Spinach

2½ cups Crescent Ridge Dairy Milk

lemon slices (optional)

- Melt butter in saucepan; saute onion until tender.
- Blend in flour and seasonings; stir and cook 3-4 minutes.
- Remove from heat; stir in chicken broth.
- Heat to boiling, stirring constantly; add carrots.
- Cook over medium heat, stirring occasionally, until carrots are tender.
- Cool to lukewarm.
- Add spinach; puree in blender.
- Stir in milk, cover and chill.
- Serve with lemon slices, if desired.
- Serves 4-5.

Polish Potato Soup

¼ cup butter
4 cups diced Tater Delight Potatoes
1 cup finely chopped celery
1 medium onion, chopped
1 pimento, minced
2 tbsp minced parsley
4 cups chicken or beef broth
1½ cups Czepiel's Sour Cream
½ tsp paprika

- In large saucepan, melt butter; saute potatoes, celery, onion and pimento.
- Add parsley and broth; simmer until vegetables are tender.
- Blend in sour cream and paprika.
- Serve immediately.
- Serves 4.

Clam Chowder

2 medium Tater Delight Potatoes
1 strip bacon
1 (8 oz) can clam juice
1 medium onion, chopped
2 cups West Lynn Creamery Light Cream
2 cups Pier 12 Chopped Clams
4 tbsp butter
salt and pepper

- Parboil potatoes until soft; dice.
- In separate pot, cook bacon until golden but not crisp.
- Remove bacon, add clam juice and onion to drippings.
- Cook until onion is transparent.
- Add cream, chopped clams, butter and potatoes.
- Simmer 10 minutes, being careful not to boil.
- Salt and pepper to taste.
- Serves 2.

Fish Chowder

3 thin slices salt pork
1 medium onion, chopped
1½ lbs Pier 12 Haddock
6 boiled potatoes
12 Bent's Common Crackers, broken into large pieces
1 qt All Star Dairy Milk
1 tsp butter
salt and pepper

- Fry salt pork and onion together. Boil fish until tender.
- Heat milk and butter in double boiler; add crackers.
- Add pork, onion, potatoes, fish, butter, salt and pepper; heat thoroughly.
- Serves 6-8.

Shiitake Mushroom Bisque

4 tbsp unsalted butter, divided

4 tbsp finely chopped onion or shallot

1 clove garlic, finely chopped

1 lb Delftree Shiitake Mushrooms, finely chopped

1 tbsp all-purpose flour

3½ cups broth (chicken, beef or vegetable)

1 sprig thyme
or
½ tsp dried thyme

½ tsp dried tarragon

½ tsp salt

½ cup West Lynn Creamery Heavy Cream

1 egg yolk

2 tbsp sherry, Madeira or Marsala

salt and freshly ground pepper

- Melt 2 tbsp butter in large skillet over medium heat.
- Add onion and garlic; cook, stirring, 5 minutes.
- Add mushrooms; cook, stirring, 10 minutes. If mushrooms stick to pan, add ¼ cup broth.
- Melt remaining butter in large saucepan over medium heat.
- Add flour; cook, stirring 5 minutes, taking care not to allow flour to brown.
- Gradually add broth, whisking constantly until smooth.
- Add mushroom mixture, thyme, tarragon and salt; simmer 30 minutes.
- Puree soup in food processor and strain through fine sieve into saucepan, rubbing solids through with wooden spoon.
- Whisk cream and egg yolk together in bowl; beat in about ½ cup hot soup.
- Add mixture to remaining soup and simmer, stirring. Do not allow to boil.
- Add sherry, Madeira or Marsala and season with salt and pepper to taste.
- Serves 4-6.

Salmon and Scallop Stew with Hard Cider and Ginger

1 lb Pier 12 Bay Scallops

1 (1 lb) Pier 12 Frozen Salmon Steak

2 cups West County Hard Apple Cider

1 cup sweet apple cider

1 tsp grated fresh ginger

2 tbsp finely julienned fresh ginger

2 cups fish or salmon stock

4 sprigs fresh thyme

1 tbsp lemon juice

salt and white pepper

½ cup Jerusalem artichokes, cut into ¼" pieces

2 small leeks, cut into thin rounds

coarsely chopped Italian parsley to garnish

- Rinse scallops and remove the cartilage from side, if attached. Trim or cut so all are same size.
- Rinse and trim salmon of all bones, skin and excess fat. Cut into chunks slightly larger than scallops.
- Combine ciders and grated ginger in large saucepan and boil until reduced by ⅓.
- Place fresh ginger in strainer or cheesecloth sack and place in saucepan with cider mixture.
- Add fish stock, thyme and lemon juice; simmer to reduce to 3 cups.
- Remove ginger and reserve; season broth with salt and pepper. Strain through fine sieve or cheesecloth into shallow pan.
- Place artichokes, leeks, ginger, scallops and salmon in broth.
- Over medium low heat, gently stir mixture until fish is thoroughly cooked, about 10 minutes; do not boil.
- Spoon evenly into warmed bowls and sprinkle with parsley.
- Serves 4.

Hearty Bean Soup

⅛ lb salt pork, diced

1 large onion, diced

6 cups water

6 cups Bean Farm Beans

½ lb Carando Heritage Kielbasa, cut into 1" pieces

2 cups diced Tater Delight Potatoes

- Saute pork and onion until slightly brown.
- Add water, beans and kielbasa.
- Bring to boil. Simmer 2 hours.
- Add potatoes and simmer additional 30 minutes.
- Serves 4.

SALADS

Historic Old Sturbridge Village

Cranberry Wreath Salad

1 (3 oz) pkg strawberry gelatin

1 cup hot water

1 (12 oz) ctn Ocean Spray Cran-Fruit™ Cranberry Orange Sauce

dash salt

1 (13.5 oz) can crushed pineapple

1 (3 oz) pkg lemon gelatin

1¼ cups boiling water

2 cups miniature marshmallows

1 (3 oz) pkg cream cheese, softened

¼ cup Cains Cholesterol Free Reduced Calorie Mayonnaise

dash salt

½ cup heavy cream, whipped

First Layer:
- Dissolve strawberry gelatin in hot water.
- Add cranberry orange sauce and salt; mix.
- Pour into 6½ cup ring mold.

Second Layer:
- Drain pineapple, reserving syrup.
- Dissolve lemon gelatin in boiling water.
- Add marshmallows and stir until melted; add reserved syrup.
- Chill until mixture is partially set.
- Blend cream cheese, mayonnaise and salt; add to marshmallow mixture.
- Stir in pineapple.
- If mixture is thin, chill until it will mound slightly when spooned.
- Fold in whipped cream.
- Pour over first layer; chill until firm. Unmold.
- Serves 10-12.

Unique Veronique Salad

3 cups torn red leaf lettuce

2 cups torn Bibb lettuce

1 endive, julienned

1 cup halved seedless green grapes

⅔ cup toasted pecan halves

⅓ cup sliced green onions

Dressing:

½ cup Czepiel's Nonfat Plain Yogurt

¼ cup Welch's White Grape Juice

½ cup crumbled bleu cheese

- To prepare dressing, in small bowl, combine yogurt and grape juice. Stir in bleu cheese.
- Chill until ready to serve.
- In large salad bowl, toss together lettuce, endive, grapes, pecans and onions.
- Serve salad with dressing on side.
- Serves 6.

Autumn Pear 'N Apple Salad

2 envs unflavored gelatin
2½ cups Lincoln Apple Juice, divided
¼ cup light brown sugar
1¼ cups pear nectar
¼ tsp cinnamon
⅛ tsp nutmeg
1 small Atkins Pear, chopped
1 small Atkins Apple, chopped
6 dried Calimyrna figs, quartered
¼ cup chopped pecans or walnuts
(optional)

- In medium saucepan, sprinkle unflavored gelatin over 1 cup apple juice; let stand 1 minute.
- Stir over low heat until gelatin is completely dissolved, about 5 minutes. Stir in brown sugar until dissolved.
- In large bowl, blend remaining apple juice, pear nectar, gelatin mixture, cinnamon and nutmeg.
- Chill, stirring occasionally, until mixture is consistency of unbeaten egg whites, about 1 hour.
- Fold in remaining ingredients.
- Pour into 6 cup mold; chill until firm, about 3 hours.
- Unmold onto serving platter.
- Serves 12.

Tomato Vinaigrette

4 large Gove Farm Tomatoes, peeled
and sliced
6 tbsp chopped fresh parsley
1 clove garlic, crushed
6 tbsp olive oil
2 tbsp The Herb Garden Opal Basil
Wine Vinegar
1 tsp salt
½ tsp dried basil
or
1 tsp fresh basil
⅓ tsp pepper

- Sprinkle tomatoes with parsley.
- Mix together remaining ingredients; pour over tomatoes and parsley.
- Chill 3 hours, tightly covered, or overnight.
- Serves 4-6.

Apple and Tarragon Salad with Watercress

2 envs unflavored gelatin

2 cups Welch's White Grape Juice, divided

1½ cups Lincoln Apple Juice

1 tbsp lemon juice

1 medium apple, thinly sliced

1 cup loosely packed watercress leaves

1 cup halved seedless green grapes

¼ cup chopped green onions

1 tbsp chopped fresh tarragon

grilled or broiled boneless chicken breasts, cut into strips

watercress leaves to garnish

- In medium saucepan, sprinkle gelatin over 1 cup grape juice; let stand 1 minute.
- Stir over low heat until gelatin is completely dissolved, about 5 minutes.
- In large bowl, blend remaining 1 cup grape juice, apple juice, gelatin mixture and lemon juice.
- Chill, stirring occasionally, until mixture is consistency of unbeaten egg whites, about 30 minutes.
- Spoon 1 cup gelatin mixture into 6 cup ring mold.
- Arrange apple slices, slightly overlapping, in bottom of mold.
- Fold watercress leaves, grapes, green onions and tarragon into remaining gelatin mixture; carefully spoon over apple slices.
- Chill until firm, about 4 hours.
- To serve, unmold onto serving platter, then fill center with chicken and, if desired, additional watercress leaves.
- Serves 8.

Cider Cole Slaw

½ cup Cains Cholesterol Free Reduced Calorie Mayonnaise

⅓ cup dill pickle juice

¼ cup honey

¼ cup Greenwood Farm Cider Syrup

1 small head cabbage, grated or chopped

- Mix together mayonnaise, dill pickle juice, honey and cider syrup.
- Toss dressing with cabbage.
- For stronger taste, allow mixture to sit longer.
- Serves 6.

Carrot Plus Three Salad

3 cups grated Fowler Farm Carrots

2 unpeeled Red Apple Farm Apples, chopped

½ cup raisins

¼ cup toasted slivered almonds

1 cup Czepiel's Nonfat Plain Yogurt

3 tbsp salad dressing

1 tbsp lemon juice

salad greens

- Combine carrots, apples, raisins and almonds in salad bowl.
- Blend together remaining ingredients and add to carrot mixture.
- Serve on salad greens.
- Serves 6.

Sliced Beet and Cucumber Salad with Creamy Herb Dressing

5 medium Berberian Farm Beets, trimmed and unpared

water

2 cucumbers, pared

Boston or Bibb lettuce

Dressing:

¾ cup sour cream

1 tbsp The Herb Garden Tarragon Wine Vinegar

1 tbsp prepared horseradish

1 tbsp sugar

1 tbsp chopped fresh tarragon

1 tbsp fresh dill

1 tbsp fresh chives

1 clove garlic, crushed

½ tsp salt

¼ tsp pepper

Hartman's Fresh Herbs (optional)

½ cup crumbled bleu cheese

- Cover beets with water in large saucepan. Bring to boil.
- Cover and simmer until tender, about 35 minutes.
- Drain; place beets in cold water; slip off skins and remove root ends.
- Slice beets and cucumbers into ¼" thick slices.
- Arrange in overlapping rows on lettuce-lined platter.
- To prepare dressing, combine all ingredients except bleu cheese; mix well.
- Spoon dressing over beets and cucumbers.
- Sprinkle with bleu cheese.
- Garnish with additional fresh herbs, if desired.
- Serves 6-8.

Tabouli and Sprouts Salad

1 cup dry bulgur wheat
1½ cups boiling water
1½ tsp salt
¼ cup fresh lemon or lime juice
1 tsp pressed, fresh garlic
3 green onions, including tops,
finely chopped
1 tbsp chopped fresh mint
or
½ tsp dried mint
1 cup chopped fresh parsley
1 (4 oz) pkg Jonathan's Munching Mix
1 cucumber, finely chopped
2 Volante Farm Tomatoes, chopped
(optional)

- Combine bulgur, boiling water and salt in bowl.
- Cover; let stand 30 minutes.
- Add remaining ingredients, blending well. At this point, mixture will be watery.
- Refrigerate 3 hours or overnight.
- Mix in chopped tomatoes, if desired.
- Serves 4-6.

Tangy Cole Slaw

1 tbsp margarine or butter
2 tbsp all-purpose flour
2 tbsp sugar
¼ tsp pepper
2 tbsp Chicama Vineyards Raspberry
Honey Poppyseed Mustard
1½ cups chicken broth
⅓ cup Chicama Vineyards White
Wine Vinegar
8 cups shredded red or green cabbage
½ cup chopped red onion

- In medium saucepan, over medium heat, melt margarine or butter.
- Blend in flour; cook 1 minute.
- Add sugar, pepper, mustard and chicken broth; cook until mixture thickens and boils. Stir in vinegar.
- Cover; refrigerate 1 hour.
- In large bowl, mix together cabbage and onion.
- Pour dressing over salad, tossing to coat well.
- Refrigerate at least 1 hour to blend flavors.
- Makes 9 cups.

German Potato Salad and Sour Cream

1 lb Tater Delight Potatoes or red
potatoes, boiled

1 tsp sugar

½ tsp salt

¼ tsp dry mustard

⅛ tsp pepper

2 tbsp The Herb Garden Thyme
Wine Vinegar

1 cup Czepiel's Sour Cream

½ cup sliced cucumbers

paprika

- Slice potatoes while still warm.
- Mix sugar, salt, mustard, pepper and vinegar.
- Add sour cream and cucumber; mix.
- Pour over potatoes and toss lightly.
- Before serving, sprinkle with paprika.
- Serve warm or cold.
- Serves 4.

French Quarter Rice Salad

1 (6 oz) pkg long grain and wild rice mix

⅔ cup La Spagnola Canola Oil

⅓ cup Chicama Vineyards French
Tarragon Wine Vinegar

1 tbsp Dijon mustard

1 clove garlic, minced

½ tsp hot pepper sauce

2 cups diced cooked Twin
Willows Turkey

1 large Andrews Farm Carrot, shredded

½ cup raisins

⅓ cup chopped green onions

½ cup toasted pecans

- Cook rice according to pkg directions. Cool slightly.
- In large bowl, combine oil, vinegar, mustard, garlic and hot sauce.
- Add rice, turkey, carrot, raisins and green onions; mix well.
- Cover; refrigerate 2-4 hours to blend flavors.
- Just before serving, stir in pecans.
- Serves 4.

Pesto Tortellini Salad

8 qts water

3 (9 oz) pkgs Trio's Tri-Color Tortellini

¾ cup firmly packed snow peas, stems removed

2 cups broccoli flowerets

2 (6 oz) jars Trio's Pesto Sauce

1 tbsp lemon juice

1 (6 oz) can black olives, pitted, drained and sliced

¾ cup sliced green peppers

¾ cup thinly sliced roasted peppers

½ cup grated Romano cheese

fresh basil leaves to garnish

- Bring water to rapid boil; cook tortellini 3 minutes; turn off heat.
- Before draining tortellini, put snow peas and broccoli in hot water 30 seconds.
- Drain completely; put in large mixing bowl.
- Add 1 jar pesto sauce, lemon juice, remaining vegetables and Romano cheese; mix well. Chill.
- Serve with more pesto, if desired, and garnish with fresh basil leaves.
- Serves 12-14.

Italian Pasta Salad

8 oz uncooked mostaccioli or ziti macaroni

2 large Bolton Orchards Tomatoes, coarsely chopped

1½ cups cooked broccoli flowerets

1 medium green pepper, chopped

1 cup Italian dressing

1 tbsp chopped fresh basil leaves

1 cup Carando Shredded Mozzarella Cheese

¼ cup Carando Grated Parmesan Cheese

- Cook macaroni according to pkg directions; drain and rinse with cold water until completely cool.
- In large salad bowl, combine tomatoes, broccoli, green pepper, dressing and basil.
- Add cheeses and macaroni, then toss lightly; cover and chill.
- Serves 4.

The Old State House, Boston

Anne Morris writes here about Worcester, Plymouth and the islands off the Cape. A Radcliffe seminar in art appreciation introduced Anne to the cultural richness of Worcester. She first visited Plymouth with her mother-in-law, a retired first grade teacher who had taught the Pilgrim story for thirty years but had never seen the historic place. Anne and her husband, a former professor, frequently make welcome retreats to Martha's Vineyard and Nantucket.

A graduate of Rice University, Columbia University Graduate School of Journalism and the University of Florida, she has written for various newspapers and magazines—"everything from *Boy's Life* to *Yoga Journal*."

WORCESTER

Worcester, the seat of the county by the same name, lies at the geographic center of New England. For years, people here have also made Worcester a cultural center. That is something you would never realize, whizzing past it on the Massachusetts Turnpike to the south. But take U.S. 290, and drive into this pleasant, hilly city for a look. Fall is a beautiful time to come, when the leaves are changing to rich yellows.

Though the second-largest city in the state, Worcester remains the kind of place where you can park and walk around. People smile and nod at you. There's a small-town politeness. Worcester has always welcomed newcomers. Some of the people who came here in the past stand tall in the nation's theatrical, musical, and political history. Others were the "huddled masses" that entered by Ellis Island—raw immigrant talent and energy.

The old Worcester cultural halls always drew the finest new theatrical talent. Jenny Lind sang here, Lola Montez danced, Rubinstein played his own compositions, Caruso sang, and the divine Sarah Bernhardt took the stage. The largest early visitor to Worcester was "Columbus," the first elephant seen in America. The oldest visitor—if you can believe P. T. Barnum's advertisement—was George Washington's nurse at 161 years old. Among the most serious were those ardent arguers for the abolition of slavery: Emerson, Frederick Douglass, and John Brown.

More recently, the heavenly music of performers such as Leontyne Price, Itzhak Perlman, and Pinchas Zuckerman has floated through Mechanics Hall on Main Street. Built in 1857 as a music hall for the city's working class, this Victorian structure underwent a restoration a few years back. It now boasts flawless acoustics. When the historic old hall was in danger of being torn down, the town rallied 'round it and found the money for its preservation. A real success story now, Mechanics Hall has won national architectural awards for its restoration. Critics call it the finest pre-Civil War concert hall in the United States.

Worcester's wealth of culture clearly resulted from the success of its industries. Even though it is not situated on a river or the coast, Worcester developed as a strong industrial center. Steam powered the city's nineteenth century factories and mills. Immigrant energy helped them grow. In the 1820s, city fathers promoted the building of a canal to Providence, to transport goods. Irish laborers came over in huge numbers to work on the canal.

Many French-Canadian mill workers came to Worcester after the Civil War. (A number of their wives originally taught crafts at the Worcester Crafts Institute, the brainchild of philanthropic women who thought their immigrant sisters could profit by developing local cottage industries.)

Blacks immigrated here from the American South. Swedish engineers and craftsmen also came after the Civil War. Other immigrants followed: Poles, Lithuanians, Italians, Greeks, Armenians, Syrians, Albanians, Chinese, East Indians, Thais. Today, ethnic churches reflect some of these different backgrounds. Every spring many churches in

Worcester host colorful ethnic festivals.

Drive just out of town and you'll start running into fruit and vegetable stands along the roadside, reminders that Worcester County is a significant agricultural center, too. Take Route 9 west to Leicester and see farm stands selling corn, onions, potatoes. Others stock homemade pickles, fresh herbs, tomatoes, cucumbers, strawberries, blueberries, peaches and dried flowers.

Farther west in Worcester County you discover neat rows of fruit trees where you can pick your own apples during early fall weekends. In winter, the same orchards, grown suddenly silent, offer trails for the cross-country skier.

Mostly, these orchards grow McIntosh apples. With a little imagination, you might see Johnny Appleseed wandering the backroads.

Some scholars say Johnny Appleseed was born in Worcester County, up in Leominster. (Others claim Springfield.) Johnny Appleseed was John Chapman, a fellow who traveled from place to place planting apple trees. Folklorist Richard M. Dorson, who vouches for Johnny's Leominster birth, describes the folk hero this way in *American Folklore*: "Barefoot, he wanders through the frontier forests of Ohio and Indiana, looking for likely places to plant his nurseries, clad in a mushpot hat and a coffeesack garment." Then Dorson separates the tale from the truth: "he was no self-made pauper who gave away apple trees and seeds and shoes to the needy, but a fairly successful businessman who accumulated twenty-two properties of nearly twelve hundred acres." But that's not what we learned as children, now is it?

The rural background of much of Worcester County, which reaches from the southern boundary of Massachusetts all the way to the New Hampshire border, goes back to the Native Americans who settled this region. The Nipmucks roamed all of Eastern Massachusetts, but the center of their territory was Worcester County. The Nipmucks farmed the land. They grew corn, beans, pumpkins, squash and tobacco. The women made beautiful baskets. The men made hoes from stone, wood, or clam shells. Using only hand tools and fire, the Indians cleared thousands of acres of wooded, rocky New England soil.

Every summer the Indians left their corn to mature and headed for the coast. There they ate clams, lobsters, oysters, and fish. Fishing was much easier than farming so they had time to play games. One was an early version of lacrosse, played with a deerskin ball stuffed with animal hair, and wooden sticks.

But they always went back to their farms. The Indians knew how to make fields productive by planting different crops in the same field. They pioneered letting fields lie fallow to make them more fertile in the future. Colonial farmers coming after them often took over these well-worked Indian fields.

Today, visitors to Worcester County can learn much about late nineteenth century farming by visiting the historic Pliny Freeman Farm at Old Sturbridge Village. One of New Englands's prime tourist attractions, the village is a vast living history museum. It's located in the town of Sturbridge on Route 20 west. Most of the forty buildings in the village never existed at this location. The developers brought in authentic original buildings—a meeting house, residences, a tavern, a blacksmith shop, and more—from different parts of New England to recreate a typical rural community of the 1830s. The Freeman Farm covers about seventy acres. It typifies the 200 or more farms you would find surrounding almost every New England town in the 1830s.

Agriculture was the basis of life then. Families worked together to raise crops and livestock for food. Anything extra, they traded or sold. A farm like this one grew field crops such as rye, corn, oats, barley, potatoes, pumpkins, and squash. There also would be a large kitchen garden for vegetables. In addition, the farm would have livestock and poultry. The Freeman Farm has oxen, cows, a small flock of sheep, a couple of pigs, and a flock of poultry.

Pliny Freeman was a real farmer who actually lived in Sturbridge in the 1800s. Today, the recreated Freeman Farm operates as a working historical farm. You can visit it and talk to the family. They may be pretty busy. Life here follows the seasons and knows no time clock. In spring the baby calves and lambs are born. By early summer, the farmer is shearing sheep with his hand clippers. Then there is the hurry to bring the hay in before the onset of summer rainstorms. All hands work to rake the hay and pitch it onto the oxcart. The oxen pull it to the barn for storage. Soon, the corn maturing in the fields will need to be harvested. Already, the women have started to prepare some of the other vegetables for storage.

Old Sturbridge Village prides itself on authenticity. Only historically accurate farm implements are used, and all the animals and crops have been back-bred to come as close as possible to what was actually there in 1830. The farmers do not pretend to gather hay. They do it. The vegetables ripen and are picked. The fences are really mended. Real work goes on, just as it once did.

Other areas of Old Sturbridge reflect the same care and attention to historic detail as the Freeman Farm. Only horsedrawn vehicles can drive on the dirt roads. All guides dress in authentic costumes and have been schooled in the roles they represent. Here you can see tinsmithing, weaving, cabinetmaking, broom making, candle dipping, pottery making and a variety of other crafts carried on as they were in the 1830s.

Old Sturbridge represents the mainstream of old New England life. Another museum, the Fruitlands at the town of Harvard (northeast Worcester County, on Route 2) deals with an offshoot.

Here Bronson Alcott, one of the Transcendentalists like Emerson, Thoreau, and Fuller, attempted a brief experiment in vegetarian communal living in the 1840s. His aim: to nourish the whole person. Along with a mystic named Charles Lane, Alcott launched a utopian community in this rural retreat. No one was to exploit the work of another creature. Alas, the experiment ended after seven months, with the members trying to pull their own plows over the rocky fields, so as not to exploit any livestock.

Louisa May Alcott, Bronson's daughter and the author of *Little Women,* later wrote about the experiment in an essay called "Transcendental Wild Oats." Today the old farmhouse serves as a museum for the

Transcendental Movement, which had its serious base in Concord.

The Shakers also had a community at Harvard for a time. A 1794 Shaker House has also been moved to Fruitlands as a museum. It displays samples of their beautifully simple furniture, their spinning, weaving, and other fine crafts. In addition, at Fruitlands you will find a museum to the American Indian and a collection of American art with emphasis on both folk art and the Hudson River School of Albert Bierstadt. There's a little something for everyone, in a beautiful hilly setting.

The best way to see Worcester County requires getting off the Turnpike and rambling on your own. Discover the Willard Clock House at Grafton, eleven miles southeast of Worcester, with its splendid collection of old timepieces in a neatly furnished historic home. Go shopping at one of the factory outlets at Uxbridge, which calls itself the woolen capital of the world. Or take a fall trip to Charlton, where the maples blaze yellow and gold. Visit one of the Nashoba Valley wineries, or stop at a candy factory or one of the pick-your-own blueberries places. See nurse Clara Barton's birthplace in North Oxford. Or take your children back to Worcester and spend a day at the New England Science Center and planetarium.

In winter, Wachusett Mountain State Reservation to the north of Worcester, offers both downhill skiing and cross-country. You will find good hiking trails here the rest of the year. Leominster State Forest, near Fitchburg and Leominster, offers even more hiking trails, plus fields of blueberries and wildflowers in season.

SAUCES

Hancock Shaker Village and the famous Round Stone Barn

Blueberry Sauce

½ cup sugar
2 cups crushed Patt's Blueberries
1 tbsp lemon juice
or
1 tsp cinnamon
¼ tsp salt
½ tsp Charles H. Baldwin &
Sons Vanilla

- Add sugar to blueberries, lemon juice and salt; mix well.
- Place in saucepan.
- Bring to boiling point; simmer 5 minutes.
- Add vanilla; chill.
- Serve over puddings, cakes or ice cream.
- Makes 2⅔ cups.

Dazzling Dessert Sauce

1 (8 oz) pkg cream cheese, softened
¼ cup powdered sugar
1 (12 oz) pkg Ocean Spray
Cran-Fruit™ Sauce

- In medium mixing bowl, beat cream cheese and sugar until fluffly.
- Stir in cranberry fruit sauce; mix thoroughly. Chill.
- Serve over pound cake, fruit or ice cream.
- Makes 2 cups.

Hot Coffee Ice Cream Sauce

1 (2.25 oz) pkg Plymouth Rock Coffee
Gelatin Dessert
⅓ cup sugar
⅓ cup water
½ tbsp butter or margarine
¼ tsp Charles H. Baldwin &
Sons Vanilla

- In small saucepan, combine coffee gelatin, sugar and water.
- Heat slowly, stirring, until gelatin is dissolved.
- Simmer 2 minutes, uncovered.
- Stir in butter and vanilla.
- Keep warm until ready to serve.
- Makes ⅔ cup.

Quick and Easy Salad Dressing

⅔ cup The Herb Garden Opal Basil,
Garlic-Dill or Chive Flower
Wine Vinegar

⅔ cup olive oil

⅓ cup water (optional)

2 tbsp chopped chives or green onions

2 tbsp sugar

1 tsp paprika

2 tbsp Worcestershire sauce

¼ tsp dry mustard

dash pepper

- Place all ingredients in jar; cover and shake well.
- Chill.
- Makes 2 cups.

Raspberry Poppy Seed Dressing

1 cup raspberries

1 tsp poppy seeds

1 tbsp Cumworth Farm Honey

1 tbsp vinegar

½ cup Cains All Natural Mayonnaise

- Puree all ingredients in food processor or blender; chill.
- Serve on tossed or fruit salads.
- Makes 1 cup.

Tasty Mustard Salad Dressing

3 tbsp olive oil

1 tbsp Chicama Vineyards Tarragon
Wine Vinegar

¼ tsp lemon juice

1 tbsp Sloan Tavern
Honeysuckle Mustard

1 tsp liquid garlic

1 tsp horbes de provence

- Place all ingredients in jar; cover.
- Shake well and serve.
- Makes ¾ cup.

Camembert Sauce

4 oz Craigston Camembert Cheese
1 cup heavy cream
¼ cup Marsala wine
dash nutmeg, salt and white pepper
⅛ tsp Hartman's Sweet Basil, Chervil or Parsley

- Melt cheese in microwave or double boiler; remove rind.
- Add remaining ingredients; stir gently until well blended.
- Serve on chicken, fish, pasta, artichokes, asparagus or broccoli.
- Makes 1¾ cups.

Marinade for Fish or Chicken

3 tbsp lemon juice
3 tbsp Greenwood Farm Cider Syrup
1½ tbsp soy sauce

- Thoroughly mix all ingredients.
- Makes ½ cup.

Tangy Barbecue Sauce

1¾ cups ketchup
1¼ cups Pepsi-Cola
4 tbsp Worcestershire sauce
2 tbsp liquid smoke
2 tbsp brown sugar
2 tbsp yellow mustard
dash hot pepper sauce

- In saucepan, blend ingredients together; simmer 30 minutes.
- Makes 3½ cups.

Simple Barbecue Sauce

1 cup ketchup
1½ tbsp Sloan Tavern Honeysuckle Mustard
1 tbsp dark brown sugar
1½ tbsp Chicama Vineyards White Wine Vinegar
1 tbsp soy sauce

- Place all ingredients in saucepan.
- Bring to boil, simmering 2-3 minutes.
- Makes 1¼ cups.

MAIN DISHES

Winter at Old Sturbridge Village

Easy Elegant Brunch

8 oz ham, thinly sliced

4 slices Freedman's Whole Wheat Bread, toasted and buttered

12 spears asparagus, partially cooked

8 oz Smith's Country Gouda, sliced

- Place ham on toast.
- Place 3 asparagus spears on each slice of toast.
- Cover with cheese.
- Bake in 375 degree oven 15-20 minutes, or until cheese melts.
- Serves 4.

Barbara's Tomato Quiche

1, 10" unbaked pie crust

3 large Bolton Orchards Tomatoes, peeled, seeded and chopped

1 medium onion, finely chopped

3 tbsp butter

1 tsp salt

1 tsp pepper

¼ tsp thyme

1 cup diced Swiss cheese

3 Johnson Poultry Farm Eggs, well beaten

1 cup Hood Light Cream

- Bake pie crust in 425 degree oven 10 minutes.
- Combine tomatoes, onion, butter, salt, pepper and thyme in saucepan.
- Cook over medium heat until mixture is reduced by half.
- Place cheese on top of crust.
- Pour tomato mixture over cheese.
- Mix eggs and cream.
- Pour over tomato mixture.
- Bake 10 minutes at 425 degrees; reduce heat to 375 degrees and bake additional 35 minutes, or until set.
- Let quiche stand a few minutes before cutting.
- Serves 5-6.

Butternut-Sausage Quiche

1, 9" unbaked pastry shell

4 Carando Sweet Italian Sausage Links

4 tbsp chopped onion

½ cup Wheeler Farm Butternut Squash, cooked and drained

salt and pepper

¼ tsp nutmeg

¾ cup grated Swiss cheese

2 Johnson Poultry Farm Eggs

1 cup West Lynn Creamery Heavy Cream

finely chopped toasted almonds (optional)

- Bake unpricked pastry shell in preheated 425 degree oven 6 minutes.
- Remove from oven, reduce temperature to 350 degrees.
- Remove casing from sausage, crumble and saute with onion; drain.
- Mash squash with salt, pepper and nutmeg.
- Spread sausage and onion mixture into bottom of shell.
- Sprinkle with cheese.
- In bowl, mix squash, eggs and heavy cream until smooth. Pour into shell over cheese.
- Sprinkle with almonds.
- Place on cookie sheet and bake 40-50 minutes, or until knife inserted in center comes out clean.
- Serves 4.

Hard Cider Casserole

1 lb pork sausage

prepared mustard

2 tart Outlook Farm Apples, sliced

2 onions, sliced

1½ tsp Hartman's Soup Herbs

½ btl West County Hard Cider

- Shape sausage into patties.
- Spread mustard over each.
- Cover with layers of apples and onions; add herbs. Pour on cider; cover.
- Bake 45 minutes at 250 degrees.
- When cooked, pour off broth and reduce heat.
- Add additional herbs to garnish.
- Serves 4-6.

Betsy's Sprout Salad Pockets

1 Berberian Cucumber
1 Berberian Zucchini
1 Berberian Summer Squash
4-6 pita bread rounds
mayonnaise
dressing
1 cup Jonathan's Sprout Salad

- Cut unpeeled cucumber, zucchini and squash crosswise into very thin slices.
- Cut pita bread in half; liberally spread entire inside with mayonnaise.
- Arrange layers of vegetables on both sides and stuff middle with sprout salad.
- Top with favorite dressing, and garnish with ½ slice of each vegetable.
- Serves 6-8.

Camembert French Bread Pizza

1 loaf Baldwin Hill French Bread, halved
1 cup Trio's Pesto
4 oz Craigston Camembert Cheese, sliced
½ red onion, thinly sliced into rings
½ cup sliced mushrooms
1 cup sun-dried tomatoes
½ green bell pepper, thinly sliced into rings
½ red bell pepper, thinly sliced into rings
½ cup sliced ripe olives
olive oil
salt and freshly ground pepper

- Spread French bread halves with pesto; top with cheese.
- Arrange onion, mushrooms, tomatoes, peppers and olives on top; drizzle with olive oil and sprinkle with salt and pepper.
- Wrap very loosely in foil.
- Bake at 325 degrees 25 minutes.
- Cut with serrated knife and serve immediately.
- Serves 2-4.

Meat Stuffed Zucchini

3, 10" Idylwilde Farm Zucchini
1 lb Diamond Cuts Ground Beef
1 onion, finely chopped
1 clove garlic, minced
1 tbsp vegetable oil
4 tbsp fine dry bread crumbs, divided
salt and pepper

- Place whole zucchini in boiling water; cook 10 minutes. Immerse in cold water until cool.
- Remove stem ends and slice lengthwise.
- Remove pulp carefully; mash or finely chop, discarding large seeds.
- Saute ground beef with onion and garlic in oil; stir and cook until meat is cooked thoroughly. Combine with 3 tbsp bread crumbs, zucchini pulp, salt and pepper to taste.
- Spoon filling into zucchini shells; sprinkle with remaining bread crumbs.
- Place in baking dish with ⅛" water; bake in 350 degree oven 15 minutes.
- Serves 6.

Chicken Cacciatore

¼ cup La Spagnola Corn Oil
1 clove garlic, minced
3 chicken breasts, halved and skinned
1 medium onion, chopped
2 tbsp chopped green pepper
4 fresh Gove Farm Tomatoes, peeled and chopped
¼ cup Chicama Vineyards Chenin Blanc
¼ tsp rosemary
1 bay leaf
¼ tsp basil
⅛ tsp pepper
cooked rice or noodles

- Heat oil in large skillet; saute garlic.
- Add chicken and brown. Remove chicken.
- Add onion and green pepper to skillet, adding more oil if necessary. Cook until tender; pour off fat.
- Return chicken to skillet. Add remaining ingredients; cover and simmer over low heat 30 minutes, or until chicken is tender.
- Remove bay leaf before serving.
- Serve over rice or noodles.
- Serves 6.

Microwave Lamb Curry

1 tbsp butter

1 cup chopped onion

2 tbsp curry powder

1½ lbs Blood Farm Boneless Lamb, cut into ½" pieces

¼ cup all-purpose flour

1 cup chicken broth

2 Bolton Spring Farm Apples, peeled and chopped

1 (8 oz) can tomatoes, drained and chopped (optional)

¼ cup Bear Meadow Farm Apple Chutney

½ cup Czepiel's Sour Cream or Plain Yogurt

chopped peanuts to garnish

3 cups hot cooked rice

- In 3 qt microwave casserole, combine butter, onion and curry.
- Cover with lid; microwave on HIGH 4 minutes, or until onion is tender, stirring once during cooking.
- In large bowl, toss lamb with flour.
- Stir lamb and flour into casserole, cover; microwave on HIGH 6 minutes, or until meat is no longer pink, stirring once during cooking.
- Stir in broth, apples, tomatoes and chutney.
- Cover; microwave on HIGH 7 minutes, or until boiling, stirring once during cooking. Stir again.
- Reduce power to 50%.
- Microwave 30 minutes, or until meat is tender, stirring 3 times during cooking.
- Let stand, covered, 5 minutes.
- Stir in sour cream.
- Garnish with peanuts; serve over rice.
- Serves 6.

Zesty Joes

1 lb Diamond Cuts Ground Beef

½ cup ketchup

1 tbsp chili powder

¾ cup Ocean Spray Cran-Fruit™ Sauce

5 Sunbeam Hamburger Buns

- In skillet, brown hamburger; drain.
- Add next 3 ingredients and heat thoroughly.
- Serve on buns.
- Serves 4-5.

Malabar Seafood Curry

½ lb snow peas

½ cup unsweetened coconut flakes

4 tbsp East India Instant India
Curry Paste

¾ tbsp peppercorns

1 tbsp Bear Meadow Farm
Garlic-Wine Vinegar

2 red bell peppers, cubed

1 cup water

1 lb uncooked Pier 12 Shrimp and
Lobster or Crabmeat, cut into 1" pieces

water or plain yogurt (optional)

parsley to garnish

- Remove stems from snow peas and cut in half.
- Dry roast coconut flakes in skillet until golden brown.
- Add curry paste, peppercorns, vinegar, snow peas, bell peppers and water; bring to boil.
- Fold in seafood; cook at high temperature, stirring constantly, until seafood turns opaque, about 5 minutes.
- Sauce will be very thick. Add water or plain yogurt to thin sauce, if desired.
- Garnish with parsley and serve hot.
- Serves 4.

Indian Pan-Fried Fish

2 Pier 12 Halibut Filets

1 tbsp slivered almonds (optional)

cooked white rice

cilantro to garnish

Marinade:

5 tbsp plain yogurt

1½ tbsp East India Instant India
Curry Paste

1½ tbsp peanut oil

pinch salt

- Mix together all marinade ingredients.
- Lay filets into marinade mixture. Marinate, refrigerated, 1-1½ hours.
- Heat non-stick skillet with oil to medium heat.
- Lay filets in skillet. Cook until fish starts to brown on underside.
- Turn filets; continue cooking, adding almonds and any remaining marinade to skillet. Turn again to coat.
- Serve with white rice and cilantro to garnish.
- Serves 2.

Skillet Scallops

2 lbs frozen Icybay Scallops, thawed
1 (7 oz) pkg pea pods
¼ cup butter or margarine
2 Bean Farm Tomatoes, cut into eighths
¼ cup water
1 tbsp cornstarch
2 tbsp soy sauce
½ tsp salt
⅛ tsp pepper
3 cups hot cooked rice
soy sauce

- Thaw frozen scallops and pea pods.
- Rinse scallops with cold water to remove any shell particles.
- Cut large scallops in half crosswise.
- Drain pea pods.
- Melt butter in 10″ fry pan.
- Add scallops; cook over low heat 3-4 minutes, stirring frequently.
- Add pea pods and tomatoes.
- Combine water, cornstarch, soy sauce, salt and pepper.
- Cook until thick, stirring constantly; add to scallop mixture.
- Serve in rice ring with soy sauce.
- Serves 6.

Super Sprout Pockets

1 head lettuce, cleaned and torn
¼ cup sliced mushrooms
¼ cup sliced olives
¼ cup chopped Idylwilde Farm Summer Squash
¼ cup chopped cucumber
¼ cup chopped Idylwilde Farm Zucchini
¼ cup chopped Bolton Orchards Tomatoes
¼ cup thinly sliced onion
¼ cup diced Cheddar cheese
1 cup diced, cooked chicken
1 (4 oz) bag Jonathan's Alfalfa with Radish Sprouts
4-6 pita bread rounds
ranch dressing

- Toss sliced vegetables with cheese and chicken.
- Cut pockets in half and open.
- Layer sprouts in bottom of each half and fill with tossed salad.
- Top with additional layer of sprouts.
- Pour dressing over each sandwich to taste.
- Serves 6-8.

THE ISLANDS

M artha's Vineyard, Nantucket, and the tiny Elizabeth Islands lie to the south of Cape Cod's elbow. No bridge connects them to the cares of the mainland. Ironically, it's this very lack of a highway link that lures hundreds of thousands of visitors every summer.

Accessible only by air and sea, these islands have kept their charm and individuality. Cuttyhunk, in the Elizabeth chain, remains the least developed, least visited of the public islands. Nantucket appears grandest and quaintest; Martha's Vineyard, the richest in variation. The islands came into being aeons ago, the final bits of land added to New England. Melting glacial ice left them behind in the Atlantic, so many new pearls in the sea.

The triangular-shaped Martha's Vineyard is the largest of the islands and the easiest to get to. The Vineyard lies only four miles from the mainland at its closest point. Yet, it seems in spirit far away, well removed from the push and pull of modern life. The forty-five minute

111

ferry ride, where gulls swoop alongside and a balmy wind whips your jacket, becomes a real voyage into yesterday. Plenty of people come for the day, only to wish they had planned to stay longer. Sometimes they return, forever.

The Vineyard's 108 square miles change from rocky bluffs and sandy beaches to rich, rolling farmland. The island is only twenty-four miles long and ten miles wide. You can easily combine an afternoon on the beach with a ride in the country. Make that a bike ride. The warm sun on your back, a soft breeze, and narrow winding roads that open onto spectacular seaside views conspire to make travel by bike the best.

Martha's Vineyard has seven townships: Edgartown, Oak Bluffs, Vineyard Haven, Gay Head, Chilmark (including Menemsha), and West Tisbury. (Ferries land at Vineyard Haven and Oak Bluffs.) The first permanent colonial settlement on the island took place in 1642, at Edgartown, which was then known as Great Harbour.

Well before that there were the Native American inhabitants, the Wampanoags and the Nausets. They built wigwam villages and cultivated fields of corn. Life was good. They feasted on sweet, wild strawberries and tangy grapes. They hunted rabbits and fished for bass. They held the first clambakes. They dug clams along the beach, and baked them in shallow pits filled with hot stones. Through the years, their feet wore deep paths into the island terrain. Always, they picked the easiest, safest and fastest routes, where the streams were shallowest, the footing surest. You can still walk these paths today. Many have become Vineyard roads. Others remain narrow, definite trails, like the Mill Path, which cuts across the island.

Read a map today and you will find Indian names on many places. The Indians were here first, and it shows. Tashmoo Lake means "Great Spring" in Wampanoag. Legend tells that an Indian set out on a journey through the forest. He was blessed with a mother who could predict the future. She foretold that near the end of his trip he would find beautiful springs of pure water. When the tired and thirsty Indian came to a lake, he rejoiced. He kneeled and drank from the snow-white shell his mother had given him. He called the lake, Tashmoo. Other stories go with other names. Menemsha, on the sea means "place of observation"; Chappaquiddick across the channel is "the separate island"; Katama is "crab fishing place" and Nobnocket, "dry place."

Englishmen first set foot on Martha's Vineyard in 1602, arriving there in a ship called the *Concord*. The story is that their captain, Bartholomew Gosnold, named the island for his baby daughter, Martha, and for the wild grapevines he found. Wild grapes no longer cover the island. Now, Martha's Vineyard has a new family-operated vineyard near West Tisbury planted with fine European grapes. On cloudy or rainy days, when the beach loses its allure, visitors line up to see how the various local wines and wine vinegars are made. They sample the familiar white zinfandel and the tempting cranberry-apple. They tour the greenhouse used for bottling and labeling. The same conditions that made this island ideal for wild grapes made it a natural for a modern-day commercial vineyard.

"Don't you like the sound of it?" our tour guide Bill asks with a smile. "A vineyard on Martha's Vineyard!"

Grapes were not the only tasty fruit Gosnold found on the islands. John Brereton, who sailed with Gosnold, reported seeing red and white strawberries on Martha's Vineyard far bigger than any in England.

Visitors to Martha's Vineyard today can pick their own strawberries most years at farms near Tisbury and West Tisbury. Families that have lived on the island "for generations and generations" grow all kinds of produce. Some they sell at roadside stands.

"We grow strawberries, lettuce, peas—sugar, shell, and snow—cucumbers, corn, beans—yellow and green—broccoli, radishes, beets, green onions, turnips, potatoes, squash—three kinds—eggplant, green peppers," one teen-aged farmer's daughter named Prudy (Yes, it's short for Prudence) told us. "We buy fruits off-island, and in the fall we have pumpkins. Our season starts in May and closes Thanksgiving. We have greenhouses where we grow cut flowers—snapdragons and zinnias. A major crop is the sweet corn. We sell it to the restaurants on the island."

The Indians first taught the settlers how to plant corn. In early island elections, corn and beans were used as ballots. Corn was FOR; beans were AGAINST. Who knows why?

The Indians also showed the Englishmen how to hunt whales from boats and tow them to the beaches, to boil out the oil. The braves paddled their canoes within range of the whale, then let fly with harpoons. It was a risky business, but success meant food for weeks. The Indians taught the settlers to fish these waters. The Englishmen raised sheep and cattle, too, brought over from the mainland. By 1720, they were exporting butter and cheese by the shipload.

It was not so easy to live on one of these islands during the American Revolution. British warships would retreat to the harbor at Vineyard Haven. The people of Martha's Vineyard supported the patriots, and at Vineyard Haven erected a liberty pole as a symbol. When the captain of a British warship arranged to buy the liberty pole from a fearful town official, three teen-aged girls risked their lives to blow up the pole. The captain sailed away in anger.

Still, the people on the Vineyard knew they had little hope of resisting if the British ever chose to attack. In 1778, a fleet of forty British warships bristling with cannon sailed into Vineyard Haven. They burned ships, destroyed fields, and carried off more than 300 oxen and 10,000 sheep, when they left four days later. The people would have starved in the harsh winter, but luckily a blizzard drove a school of sea bass into the lagoon pond. People from all over the island came to cut frozen fish from the ice.

Before the Revolution, Edgartown was the home port for whaling ships that sailed the North Atlantic. The war stopped this prosperous trade. Only in the 1820s did the whaling industry recover. How well it recovered can be seen today in the grand white houses built in Edgartown by the masters of whaling ships. Many houses have widow's walks, railed platforms built into the roofs, where wives could watch the sea for ships returning from voyages three and four years long. These white-columned, dark shuttered Greek revival houses line

Water Street, facing the harbor.

Whaling lingers as a sentimental symbol of the Vineyard. Whales and sailing ships appear on signs of everything from inns to realty offices. The island calls visitors to celebrate "A Whale of a Christmas" with carriage rides, wreath making and Christmas parades.

A different kind of heritage lives in Oak Bluffs. It began here in 1835, when the Edgartown Methodists held a camp meeting in a grove of huge oak trees near the bluff that overlooks Vineyard Sound. They slept in large tents—women on one side of a canvas partition, men on the other—and attended day-long church services and sermons held in a circus tent.

By 1859, the Martha's Vineyard Camp Meeting Association had its own building, and Victorian gingerbread cottages had begun to replace the tents. These gaily painted cottages cluster tightly around a cone-shaped, open-air iron Tabernacle, where services were held daily. A further distinction of Oak Bluffs is that it is the site of one of the oldest black resorts in America.

President Ulysses S. Grant attended the "Grand Illumination Night" one year at Oak Bluffs. Still an annual custom, this is the evening in August when all the cottagers hang numbers of old-time Japanese lanterns from their porches, and light them all at once, to a signal of, "Let the lanterns be lit!" They illuminate the entire campground with a wondrous glow.

At Oak Bluffs children can ride on the oldest carousel still in operation in the country. It once graced Coney Island. Designated a National Historic Landmark, the Flying Horses Carousel was hand-carved in New York City in 1876. It's still open every day in summer and on weekends in spring and fall.

The towns of Vineyard Haven and Tisbury provide one of the busiest harbors on the island, where most of the ferries dock. Vineyard Haven has a contemporary look, since much of its historic architecture was lost in the great fire of 1883, when seventy-two buildings in a forty-acre area burned. The Tisbury Museum in the 1796 Ritter House on Beach Road shows what life was like here in the nineteenth century. These days, Vineyard Haven is a gathering place for New York and Washington intellectuals, and a less formal setting than Edgartown. Vineyard Haven is the busiest town on the island, its commercial center. But you will also find here the largest collection of resident wooden boats of any port in the Northeast. It's a safe haven. Gratia Eldridge recalled this old saying in her reminiscences of growing up there in the late 1800s.

> *"There is a sailor's hell,*
> *There is a sailor's heaven;*
> *One is Nantucket Shoals,*
> *The other is Vineyard Haven.*
> **—from The Captain's Daughters**
> **of Martha's Vineyard.**

The port of Menemsha toward the west end of the island looks and feels like a fishing village. Weathered buildings and a serviceable dock let you know this place is real, not only a background for picture post cards, though it's certainly on plenty of those. The popular fish markets here sell in season pounds of swordfish, lobster, scallops, flounder, striped bass and bluefish. Menemsha's commercial fishermen come from families who have lived off the sea for hundreds of years.

One claim to fame Menemsha pays but slight attention to is that of home port to one of the world's great adventurers. For a time in the early 1900s, Joshua Slocum, the first man to sail alone around the world, kept his sloop, *The Spray,* at Menemsha harbor. He lived inland himself, near Tisbury. He took a turn at growing hops but later gave that up to go to sea again. He made various voyages out of Menemsha. He disappeared on a daring voyage to the jungles of South America.

The people of the Vineyard never made much of a fuss about Slocum. He might be famous, but he was just another person passing through. Over the years many famous people have made the Vineyard their sometime home. These include Walter Cronkite, Jacqueline Onassis, William Styron, Beverly Sills, Carly Simon, Garson Kanin, Spike Lee, Edward Bennett Williams, and many others. Year-round residents do their best to give them no special treatment. To the Vineyard, fame is fleeting. Nature endures. What matters are places like Gay Head.

Here, colorful mile-long cliffs rise sixty feet above the sea at the westernmost tip of the island. Best viewed at sunset, the cliffs make a rainbow of natural colors—blue, tan, grey, red, white, and orange—in their striated layers of clay. Gay Head has long been an attraction, though it can be a dangerous rocky place for ships. The old Gay Head Lighthouse dates to 1799.

Around the turn of the century, an excursion boat took people from Oak Bluffs to Gay Head. There the Indians met them in an ox cart for the tour. Herman Melville's character Tashtego was a Gay Head Indian. The author described the area as "the most westerly promontory of Martha's Vineyard, where there still exists the last remnant of a village of red men, which has long supplied the neighboring island of Nantucket with many other most daring harpooners." These Indians once made pottery from the clay of the cliffs, but concern about erosion has halted that.

From the top of the cliffs you can see Cuttyhunk to the north. It's a small patch of land some fourteen miles off the mainland. Cuttyhunk is the only one of the Elizabeth Islands accessible to the public by a ferry, which comes only once a day even at the height of the summer tourist season. That adds to the feeling of isolation, plus the fact that most of the other Elizabeth islands are privately owned, not places you can visit. About forty people live on Cuttyhunk year-round. They make their living by odd jobs or by taking out fishermen after the bass that live between the islands. Bartholomew Gosnold landed here first before reaching Martha's Vineyard.

A stone tower at one end of the island marks the first English habitation on the coast of New England. Gosnold found wild sassafrass growing on the island and planned to make a plantation here. He left some members of his crew behind and went off to explore another of the Elizabeth Islands. But he did not return when expected, and food supplies ran out. By the time he did return, the hungry crew wanted nothing more to do with Cuttyhunk.

Gosnold also visited Nantucket, eighteen miles to the east of Martha's Vineyard. The Wampanoag Indians who first settled there called it "Land Far Off at Sea," and *Canopache*, "The Place of Peace." Its distance from shore—thirty miles south of Cape Cod—has made it a special place. Writers outdo themselves trying to describe the triangular shape of Nantucket, which is fourteen miles long and averages three and one-half miles wide. Melville called it "an anthill in the sea." Others have said the island looks like a blunted harpoon, a teardrop, a crescent, a porkchop, a sailor's hammock suspended from its hooks in a whaler's cabin, and an ivory arm in a sapphire sea.

Nantucket, with its windswept moors and miles of gleaming beaches, its cobblestone streets and elegant houses, cries out for more creative description. Warmed by the Gulf Stream and swathed in summer fogs, it can seem as mysterious and faraway as the setting for a novel.

Melville described Nantucket again and again in *Moby Dick*. He wrote:

> "*Nantucket! Take out your map and look at it. See what a real corner of the world it occupies; how it stands there, away off shore, more lonely than the Eddystone lighthouse. Look at it—a mere hillock, and elbow of sand; all beach, without a background.*"—**Chapter Fourteen**

Elizabeth Oldham, director of tourism for the island, calls Nantucket quite simply "one of the most beautiful spots on earth." One of the 7,000 people who live year-round on this sandy mound, she would speak warmly of it even if it were not her job.

"I worked in New York for years," she said, "but my family had always been here, and I had a second home here. Now that Nantucket has become my permanent home, I leave the island very rarely. I like its size, its smallness, the way it can be encompassed. Its natural beauty is a glory. Did you know that one-third of the land here is in conservation hands? It will be forever wild."

Forever wild means there will always be moors, with bayberry, huckleberry, shadblow, and wild heather. Acres of wild grapes perfume the air in autumn. Shy little white flowers called Quaker-ladies appear in summer, along with other delicate blossoms. Many of the plants on Nantucket come from far away: ivy from England, heather and broom from Scotland, the rugosa rose from Japan. Sea captains brought some of them; the wind, others.

Year-round, three hundred white-tailed deer roam free on the island, hidden by the brush. They trace their ancestry to a lone buck found swimming near shore in 1922, and two does later brought from Michigan to be his simple harem. Rabbits, pheasants, and woodcock hurry for cover here; wild ducks fly overhead, and bluefish swim in the harbor. Harbor seals winter nearby. Some twenty-five live off the neighboring island of Muskeget, a quiet haven. The Nantucket Conservation Foundation, the Massachusetts Audubon Society, and other conservation groups do what they can to keep the outlying areas timeless and unchanged.

Yet, nature is not without its bounty. Nantucket is famous for its cranberries and has the largest bog in the world. Nantucket sea captains carried cranberries along on their voyages to ward off scurvy. Today, the Nantucket Conservation Foundation owns the bogs on the island and leases them out. In June and July, tiny light-pink flowers cover the cranberry bushes and color the bogs in endless waves. Each fall the bogs are flooded. Machines come in to harvest the tart, purplish berries. About 3,000 one-hundred pound barrels are shipped annually.

Nantucket may be even more famous for another of nature's gifts, the small, delectable bay scallop. Dragging for scallops is a hard way to make a living, but in a good year it brings in between two and three million dollars to the local economy. Half of all the bay scallops harvested in Massachusetts come from Nantucket waters.

No Nantucket towns are very far from the sea. Quaint, perfect places, they look like living history museums. Better than that, they are real. The village of Siasconset (called mostly 'Sconset), on the eastern end of the island, began as an Indian fishing village. In the seventeenth century, fishermen built tiny cottages here out of wood left from shipwrecks or brought out from town.

Today the crowded-together gray cottages look like Wales. Some have blue shutters. Tradition holds that these were the houses of captains and first mates. Later, people built more cottages like the first ones. Bright hollyhocks still grow in their gardens, and wild roses cascade over the doorways. A sign on the bluff points out over the ocean and says: "To Spain and Portugal, 3000 miles."

Who could blame people for wanting to see the mother of pearl shades of the sunrise off 'Sconset? In the late 1800s, a little narrow gauge railroad ran out from Nantucket, bringing Broadway here. Stars like Lillian Russell and Joseph Jefferson came.

Another less-traveled fishing village, Wauwinet, also began as a collection of fishermen's huts, just four miles down the curving beach from Great Point Lighthouse, where waves crash together at the end of a narrow spit of land.

The historical feel of Nantucket is not limited to such tiny villages. The town of Nantucket itself could be from the eighteenth century, except for the telephone wires. More than 400 of its houses were built before 1830. A few function as museums, but most are places where people get up, have breakfast, and go forth. No other town in America has so many old houses. All of the town of Nantucket has been designated a National Historic Landmark.

Every spring the town gathers around Main Street to celebrate the end of winter with a daffodil festival and parades. Every store window displays bright yellow daffodils. Nantucketers dress up in vintage costumes to drive antique cars through the town. They end with an elegant tailgate picnic at Sconset.

Whaling created the boom that led to much of Nantucket's wealth. The world wanted whale oil to fuel its lamps, and Nantucket could provide it. The town geared itself to the whaling industry, even paved the streets with cobblestones to keep the whale oil drays from sinking into the mud.

Melville wrote of the hardy Nantucket seamen: "What wonder, then, that these Nantucketers, born on a beach, should take to the sea for a livelihood! They first caught crabs and quahaugs in the sand; grown bolder, they waded out with nets for mackerel; more experienced, they pushed off in boats and captured cod; and at last, launching a navy of great ships on the sea, explored this watery world (for whales)."

But the last of the mighty whaling ships, *The Oak,* sailed out of Nantucket harbor in 1869. Nantucket suffered a series of unrelated setbacks that ended its days as whaling capital. First, the Great Fire of 1846 destroyed the entire waterfront. Then, only a few years later, the California Gold Rush drew seamen west to seek their fortune. Around the same time, larger ships were built demanding a deeper harbor. New Bedford took over from Nantucket. And once kerosene replaced whale oil as the fuel of choice, the future of Nantucket definitely dimmed. Without whaling, what was there?

A hundred or so years later, Nantucket has found the answer in the tourist trade. The economic bust that halted all development for so long proved to be a boon. Nothing changed, and that is just the way the mainlanders like it. There is a certain pleasure in the assurance of an authentic eighteenth century street, a joy in the lonely cries of seagulls that punctuate the day more often than motorcars. Nantucket became a prime resort: for resting, swimming, sailing, playing tennis, biking, fishing, antiquing, or simply strolling. Each year "the little gray town by the sea" swells to around 40,000. Tourists come by the boatload. They are drawn by the distinctive atmosphere, the miles of beaches, the promise of wild nature, and the opportunity to reconnect with a unique past.

At first part of the Plymouth royal grant, Nantucket was bought by Thomas Mayhew, who also owned Martha's Vineyard. He sold nine-tenths of Nantucket to nine others, for "Thirty Pounds in good Merchantable Pay and Two Beaver Hats, one for myself and one for my wife" in 1659. The first white settlers came to Nantucket because they wanted to escape Puritan domination in Amesbury and Salisbury. They farmed, fished, and raised sheep.

Later, many of them turned to whaling.

The Old Mill, an old-style windmill that grinds corn with ancient machinery and grinding stones, dates to those days. Built in 1746, for the town of Nantucket, it still operates. Families used to watch from this hill for their first sight of returning whaling ships.

About this time, Quakers visited the island. The religion they brought spread rapidly here. It appealed to the independent character of the Nantucketers. The first Friends meeting was held in 1704; the first meeting house was built seven years later. For 125 years the Quakers, in the square-toed shoes and homespun clothing, dominated Nantucket. The Quakers contributed greatly to the community and family effort that made Nantucket a whaling center. Those who worked on shore making the barrels for whale oil and sewing the sails for ships had brothers and cousins out pursuing the whales.

One of the famous stories of Nantucket tells of a maiden who waited faithfully for forty years for her fiance to return from a whaling voyage on the *Zone*. She refused to accept the fact that he had been swept overboard. Instead, she went to the dock year after year, looking for Philip Coffin. One day, she caught her death of cold going to the wharf in a storm. On her death bed she cried out in happiness, "The *Zone* is in! Philip is with me at last."

All the islands have plenty of stories to tell. A rich folklore of sea chanteys, Indian legends, and tales of shipwreck and romance await those who pay a visit.

MEATS & FISH

The early-morning solitude of Nantucket

Apple and Veal Scallop

2 large Carlson Orchards Apples,
peeled, cored and sliced

¼ cup lemon juice

½ cup all-purpose flour

1 tsp salt

freshly ground pepper

8 veal medallions

¼ cup margarine

½ cup Carlson Orchards Apple Cider

1 cup Hood Whipping Cream,
unwhipped

- In medium bowl, combine apples and lemon juice; set aside.
- In paper or plastic bag, combine flour, salt and pepper.
- Add veal, a few at a time; shake to coat.
- In large skillet, brown veal on both sides in margarine; remove from skillet and set aside.
- Stir in apple mixture and cider, scraping bottom of skillet.
- Cook 3-5 minutes.
- Slowly add cream, stirring constantly.
- Simmer 5-10 minutes, or until slightly thickened.
- Add veal; heat thoroughly.
- Serves 4.

Medallions of Veal with Tomatoes and Shiitake Mushrooms

1¼ lbs veal

4 Bolton Orchards Tomatoes

2 lbs Delftree Shiitake Mushrooms

3 oz white wine

1 clove garlic

4 oz beef broth

salt and pepper

- Cut veal into 2 oz medallions and pound flat.
- Scald tomatoes in boiling water 30 seconds; remove peels.
- Cut tomatoes in half, remove seeds and dice.
- Slice mushrooms and stems.
- Saute veal until golden brown; turn and add mushrooms, tomatoes, wine and garlic.
- Simmer until heated through.
- Add beef broth, salt and pepper and reduce heat.
- Serves 4.

Swiss Veal Delight

1 lb veal round, ½" thick
6 thin slices Carando Prosciutto
6 thin slices Swiss cheese
1 cup all-purpose flour
2 large eggs, slightly beaten
½ cup milk
2 cups finely crushed State Line Potato Chips
½ cup butter
2 tbsp finely minced chives
hot cooked rice

Sauce:

½ cup butter
1 cup finely crushed State Line Potato Chips
1 tsp instant onion flakes
1 tsp salt
1 tsp MSG
¼ tsp white pepper
2 cups Czepiel's Sour Cream

- Have butcher cut veal into 6 equal portions; pound very thin, about ⅛" thick.
- Place 1 slice of prosciutto and cheese on each slice of veal.
- Roll meat as for a jelly roll, tucking in sides, and pressing ends to seal well.
- Mix together egg and milk.
- Roll each portion of meat in flour, then dip in egg mixture.
- Carefully roll each piece in finely crushed potato chips.
- Heat butter in heavy skillet; saute veal until golden brown, about 10-15 minutes, turning once.
- To make sauce, melt butter in heavy skillet; carefully stir in potato chips, onion flakes, salt, MSG and white pepper.
- Cook over low heat 5 minutes.
- Stir in sour cream; continue to cook 10 minutes, stirring gently.
- Place veal rolls on warm large platter.
- Spoon sauce on rolls; sprinkle chives on top.
- Serve with rice.
- Serves 6.

Cranberry Pot Roast

2 tbsp all-purpose flour
1 tsp Mrs. G's Herb Salt
1 tsp onion salt
¼ tsp Mrs. G's Herb Pepper
1 (3-4 lb) beef pot roast
2 tbsp shortening
4 Hartman's Whole Cloves
1, 2" Hartman's Stick Cinnamon
½ cup water
1 (16 oz) can Ocean Spray Whole Cranberry Sauce
1 tbsp vinegar
2 tbsp water

- Combine flour, salt, onion salt and pepper; rub into pot roast, using all flour mixture.
- In Dutch oven, slowly brown meat on both sides in hot shortening.
- Remove from heat; add cloves, cinnamon and ½ cup water.
- Cover tightly; simmer 2½ hours, or until tender, adding water if necessary. Spoon off fat.
- Mix cranberry sauce, vinegar and 2 tbsp water; add to meat.
- Cover; cook 10-15 minutes more.
- Remove cinnamon; spoon off fat and pour pan juices into serving dish.
- Place roast on serving platter; serve with pan juices.
- Serves 6-8.

Apple Meatloaf

2½ lbs Diamond Cuts Ground Beef
1½ cups stuffing mix
2 cups finely chopped Bluebird Acres Apples
3 Hillside Farm Eggs
2 tsp salt
2 tbsp prepared mustard
1 large onion, minced
3 tbsp prepared horseradish
¾ cup ketchup

- Combine all ingredients; mix thoroughly.
- Pack into greased 8" x 5" loaf pan.
- Bake at 350 degrees 1¼ hours.
- Serves 8-10.

Prosciutto Veal Rolls Italiano

¼ lb butter

1 lb fresh mushrooms

½ tsp salt

¼ tsp Mrs. G's Herb Pepper

2 tbsp dried parsley

¾ cup Chicama Vineyards Chardonnay

¾ cup dry vermouth

6 veal cutlets, thinly sliced

6 slices Carando Prosciutto, thinly sliced

6 slices Swiss cheese, thinly sliced

½ cup all-purpose flour

¼ tsp thyme

¼ tsp savory

1 tsp garlic powder

- Preheat oven to 350 degrees.
- Melt butter in saucepan.
- Wash mushrooms in warm water; slice; drain thoroughly.
- Place mushrooms in melted butter over moderate heat.
- Add salt, pepper and parsley; saute 15 minutes until mushrooms start to turn brown. Pour excess butter into frying pan and reserve.
- Add white wine and vermouth to mushrooms.
- Cover and cook over low heat 15 minutes longer.
- Pound cutlets; add 1 slice prosciutto and 1 slice Swiss cheese per cutlet; roll and insert toothpick to hold.
- In shallow dish, mix flour, thyme, savory and garlic powder; roll each cutlet in flour mixture until covered.
- In reserved butter, saute prosciutto-veal rolls until golden brown. If necessary, add more butter.
- Place rolls in casserole; pour on mushrooms and wine sauce.
- Bake, covered, 30 minutes, or until tender enough to pierce with fork.
- Serves 6.

Barbecued Pork Chops

1½ cups Dixie & Nikita's Wicked Awesome Barbecue Sauce

¾ cup Bear Meadow Farm Apple, Cranberry or Rhubarb Chutney

4 pork chops, 1½" thick

- Preheat oven to 350 degrees.
- Mix barbecue sauce and chutney in small saucepan; simmer 15 minutes.
- Pour over pork chops; bake 1 hour.
- Serve extra sauce on the side.
- Serves 3-4.

Left-Over Holiday Ham

½ cup all-purpose flour
1 tbsp cloves
4 tbsp Sloan Tavern Mustard
½ cup Peaceful Meadows Milk
4 ham slices
1 cup sherry

- Make paste of first 4 ingredients.
- Place ham slice in baking dish; coat with paste.
- Bake at 350 degrees until crust forms, adding sherry when crust hardens.
- Serves 4.

Mustard Chicken

½ cup Sloan Tavern Honeysuckle Mustard
2 tbsp Nashoba Valley Upland White Wine
1 cup grated Parmesan cheese
1 cup Italian seasoned bread crumbs
3 lbs boneless chicken breasts

- Thin mustard with wine to dipping consistency.
- Generously dip or soak chicken pieces in mustard mixture.
- Combine cheese and bread crumbs.
- Coat chicken pieces with crumb mixture.
- Bake at 375 degrees 45 minutes in greased pan.
- Serve hot or cold.
- Serves 6-8.

Wicked Awesome Dixie Chicken

4 chicken breasts
1 cup Dixie & Nikita's Wicked Awesome Barbecue Sauce
½ cup honey mustard
½ cup Madeira wine
2 cups hot cooked rice or noodles

- Preheat oven to 350 degrees.
- Mix together all ingredients; pour over chicken in roasting pan.
- Bake 45 minutes.
- Serve cooking sauce on side with rice or noodles.
- Serves 4.

Chicken Breasts in Mushroom Wine Sauce

3 tbsp butter, divided

3 whole chicken breasts, boned, skinned and halved

salt and pepper

3 cups sliced Delftree Shiitake Mushrooms

1 cup Nashoba Valley Baldwin Wine

½ cup condensed chicken broth

1½ tsp tarragon

¾ cup Cooper's Hilltop Farm Whipping Cream

2 tbsp all-purpose flour

chopped fresh parsley to garnish

- Heat 2 tbsp butter in large skillet.
- Season chicken breasts with salt and pepper.
- Saute chicken breasts until golden on each side.
- Remove chicken from skillet.
- Saute mushrooms in remaining butter in same skillet 2-3 minutes until almost tender.
- Add wine, broth and tarragon to skillet.
- Arrange chicken breasts on top of mushrooms in skillet.
- Cover and simmer until chicken is tender, about 10 minutes.
- Remove chicken breasts to warm serving platter.
- Combine cream and flour.
- Reduce wine mixture in skillet slightly.
- Add cream mixture and cook until mixture has thickened slightly.
- Spoon sauce over chicken.
- Garnish with parsley.
- Serve immediately.
- Serves 6.

Chicken with Red Grapes

2 tbsp olive oil

1 large red onion, thinly sliced

6 chicken breast halves, boned and skinned

⅔ cup Welch's Red Grape Juice

⅛ tsp freshly ground pepper

⅛ tsp crushed rosemary

1 cup seedless red grapes

⅔ cup West Lynn Creamery Heavy Cream

1 tbsp paprika

- Heat oil in large skillet over medium high heat.
- Saute onion in oil 1 minute.
- Add chicken; saute on both sides until golden brown.
- Reduce heat to medium; pour in red grape juice.
- Cover and cook 5 minutes.
- Add pepper, rosemary, grapes and heavy cream; continue cooking until heated through, about 5 minutes.
- Transfer chicken and grapes to heated serving platter using slotted spoon.
- Continue cooking sauce until reduced by half.
- Pour sauce around chicken; sprinkle chicken with paprika.
- Serves 6.

Lemon Chicken

2½ lemons, juiced

2 tbsp water

8 chicken breasts, boned and skinned

2 tbsp butter

1 tbsp olive oil

1 cup Green Friedman All-Purpose Flour

¼ tsp salt

¼ tsp pepper

¼ cup Greenwood Farm Cider Syrup

2 tbsp grated lemon peel

1-2 lemons, thinly sliced

- Combine lemon juice and water and marinate chicken several hours, turning periodically; reserve marinade.
- Preheat oven to 350 degrees.
- Put butter and olive oil in baking dish; place in oven until butter melts.
- Combine flour, salt, pepper; coat chicken.
- Mix syrup with grated lemon peel; spread over chicken in baking pan.
- Cover with reserved marinade.
- Put 1 lemon slice on each chicken breast and bake 35 minutes.
- Serves 8.

Lobster Newburg

4 tbsp butter

1 lb Slade Gorton & Co. Lobster Meat, cubed

1½ tbsp paprika

6 tbsp sherry

salt

white pepper

2 egg yolks, beaten

4 slices Au Bon Pain Bread, toasted

Cream Sauce:

3 tbsp butter

3 tbsp all-purpose flour

1½ cups Shady Oaks Farm Milk

¾ tsp salt

- Melt butter slowly; stir in flour and heat until bubbly.
- Add milk gradually; stir quickly until smooth.
- Cook, stirring constantly, until mixture boils and thickens.
- Remove from heat; set aside.
- In large skillet, melt butter over low heat.
- Add lobster meat and paprika; saute until golden color.
- Add sherry; simmer until wine is absorbed into lobster meat.
- Add cream sauce, salt and white pepper to taste. Stir well with a wooden spoon for 3 minutes.
- Remove from heat; add yolks of eggs, stirring briskly.
- Serve immediately on toast points.
- Serves 4.

Honey's Baked Fish Filets

2 tbsp light mayonnaise

1 tbsp Sloan Tavern Hot Mustard

1 lb Pier 12 Scrod Filets

¼-½ cup seasoned bread crumbs

¼-½ cup crushed Grainfield's® Corn Flakes

2 tbsp toasted wheat germ

½ tsp salt

½ tsp pepper

lemon and melted butter

- Combine mayonnaise and mustard; dip fish to coat.
- Combine remaining ingredients; roll fish in mixture to cover.
- Bake at 350 degrees 20 minutes, drizzling with lemon and butter to taste.
- Serves 4.

Cod Fish Florentine

1 lb fresh spinach, washed and trimmed
1½ lbs Icybay Cod Filets
3 tbsp lemon juice
salt and pepper
½ cup water
½ cup All Star Dairy Milk
2 tbsp instant blending flour
1 tbsp minced parsley
pinch nutmeg
6 tbsp grated Parmesan cheese

- Preheat oven on broil.
- Place spinach in covered pan and cook 2-3 minutes; drain well.
- Arrange fish in single layer in baking dish.
- Sprinkle with lemon juice, salt and pepper.
- Add water, cover with foil and bake 350 degrees 5-7 minutes.
- Drain liquid into saucepan; heat to boil.
- Combine milk and flour; stir into liquid.
- Cook, stirring constantly, until thickened.
- Stir in parsley, nutmeg and additional salt and pepper, if desired.
- Arrange fish in center of baking pan, surround with spinach.
- Pour sauce over all and sprinkle with cheese.
- Broil until bubbly.
- Serves 4-6.

Smelts with Beer Batter

3 Pine Hill Farm Eggs
½ can cold beer
1 tsp salt
½ cup all-purpose flour
½ cup Gray's Corn Meal
1 tsp salt
1 lb Icybay Smelts, cleaned, rinsed and dried

- Beat together eggs, beer and salt until fluffy; set aside.
- Combine flour, corn meal and salt.
- Dip smelt first into liquid batter, then into dry mixture, and back into liquid batter.
- Fry in deep fat until light brown.
- Serves 4.

PLYMOUTH

Most people these days think everyone who arrived on *The Mayflower* was a Pilgrim seeking religious freedom. In fact, only forty one were Puritans escaping religious persecution. The other sixty-one passengers came as ordinary settlers in search of better economic opportunities than England had to offer. The original plan had been to sail to an area near the Hudson River, then called "Northern Virginia." They ended up on the New England coast instead. The Pilgrims may have felt that this area would provide them more freedom than the Virginia Company. The final choice of Plymouth came after an unsuccessful attempt to cross the Nantucket Shoals and sail south. They found themselves forced back to Cape Cod. Exploring, they found the site for Plymouth.

In a historic decision to work together, both the Pilgrims and settlers aboard ship—the Saints and the Strangers—signed an agreement called the Mayflower Compact at Provincetown Harbor. They agreed to "combine ourselves together into a civill body politick." By this they gave authority to elect leaders and set their colony on a firm foundation.

The town of Plymouth lies about an hour southwest of Boston, on U.S. Highway 3. Even if you learned the Pilgrim story perfectly in school, a visit to Plymouth will give it new meaning. A life-sized replica of the Pilgrim ship, called *Mayflower II,* is docked in the harbor next to Water Street, as if this were the seventeenth century. The ship is short like the original *Mayflower,* just 104 feet long. Dark brown with red strapwork and a picture of a May-blooming hawthorn flower on the stern, the *Mayflower II* looks real enough to cross the ocean. It did, in fact, sail to Plymouth from England in 1957. A tour on board quickly creates a feel for what cramped quarters the Pilgrims suffered during their voyage of more than two months' "beating at sea."

The passengers spent most of the sixty-seven day voyage crowded below decks in a dark space that smelled of old leaky wood, tar, and too many people. For food they had only dried fish, cheese, salted beef, and hardtack. Aboard this living museum, costumed sailors and passengers aboard this living museum speak in the roles of specific people who sailed on *The Mayflower.*

Almost as soon as colonists came to the New World, some dooms-dayers back in England began to spread stories about the dangers here. The colonial sponsors fought back with tales of their own. Richard M. Dorson, a noted American folklorist, tells how a spokesman for the Council of New England countered one of the rumors about starvation in Plymouth in 1628.

There was a report that a man named Chapman had starved to death. Yes, he did, the spokesman said, but there was a reason. Chapman spent seven to eight pounds weekly on wine, tobacco, and women while his ship lay at anchor in Plymouth. On the voyage he exchanged a fifty-shilling suit for a pipeful of tobacco. Finally, he became a servant to his own servant. The servant offered Chapman a biscuit cake a day if he worked, and half a cake if he preferred to be idle. Chapman chose to be idle and starved to death. "Where was the fault now, in the man or in the country?"

A few steps away from the *Mayflower II*, Plymouth Rock rests beneath a protective canopy, a rectangular Greek monument with white columns. Most people come expecting a huge boulder beneath this temple-like canopy. Instead, they look down and see a smallish white rock inscribed with the date, 1620. The size of the rock comes as a shock. Still, it is impressive. Here, on this rock, the Pilgrims first stepped ashore. A guide explains that the rock used to be four or five times larger. Sea and wind took its toll.

Souvenir hunters also have carted bits of Plymouth Rock away through the years. One small piece of the rock rests at an oil refinery in Hull, England. Another recently found a home in The Smithsonian Institution after spending years as the doorstep of Plymouth's Harlow House, built in 1677 and now a museum. Even the early Patriots carried off a piece of Plymouth Rock just before the Revolution. That, however, was returned in 1880, the year the canopy was built. These days, the Commonwealth of Massachusetts watches over Plymouth Rock.

For a time, historians debated whether Plymouth Rock deserved its reputation as the first place the Pilgrims stepped ashore in the New World. Some scholars pointed out that contemporary accounts of early days in the colony made no mention of Plymouth Rock. Others believed Elder Faunce, who, in 1741 at age 95, identified this rock as the Pilgrims' stepping stone. He said his father had pointed it out to him. Deposited by a glacier, the rock sits higher than the rest of the beach. It made a natural stepping stone.

Across Water Street from Plymouth Rock stands Coles Hill, the site of secret burials. The first winter a great many Pilgrims died. Rainy, miserable weather made it hard to bounce back from the rigors of the ocean voyage. Many had caught scurvy and ship fever. Those who were sick got sicker. Six died in December, eight in January, seventeen in February, thirteen in March. Half of the original group, in fact, died that first year. At that point, the colonists lived in deadly fear of the Indians. There had been one skirmish, and they thought the Indians might attack in earnest if they knew how many of the colonists had died. As a precaution, the survivors buried their dead at night in secret graves on Coles Hill. For cover, they planted rows of corn over the graves.

The story goes that one group of Indians plotting to kill the English in Plymouth for their provisions, gave up when they saw the guard reading the Bible. His face looked so serious that they thought he must have learned of their scheme from his holy book.

Friendship with the Indians only began the day that Samoset, a visiting chief, walked into the colonial village and said, "Welcome." He introduced the Pilgrims to Massasoit (the Wampanoag chief whose towering statue stands today on Coles Hill) and to Squanto, a Patuxet Indian. They helped the colonists learn to use the land. Squanto taught them how to plant corn, placing a herring in each hole for fertilizer. He showed them how to trap eels, and how to tap the maple trees for sap. The colony began to succeed in the New World, with the help of their new Indian friends.

Fall brought fine crops. The colonists held a harvest festival. It was not the same thing as Thanksgiving at all. A harvest festival meant singing and dancing and feasting. Thanksgiving, for the Pilgrims, was a holy day of fasting and prayer, held when times were especially good. But, nowadays, the folks at Plymouth humor the popular notion. Like us, they celebrate Thanksgiving with a harvest feast. That first fall harvest festival lasted three days. Colonists hunted ducks, geese, and turkeys for it, and the Indians provided venison—five deer. They also feasted on sea bass and cod, and corn bread. They prepared it all in the fireplace, over an open fire.

Today you can experience the way the colonists lived, at Plimoth Plantation. (They spell "Plymouth" that way because Governor William Bradford spelled it with an "i" in his written history. In those days, spelling was not something fixed.) This non-profit museum, like the *Mayflower II,* dramatically recreates their world. A cluster of sixteen wooden houses surrounded by a stockade, the village is a living history museum, authentic in its details. Even the breeds of livestock have been back-bred to produce the kinds of animals the Pilgrims would have had:

old breeds of chicken, a Dartmoor pony, and lineback cattle.

An Irishman expert supervised thatching of the roofs on the Pilgrim huts. Reeds gathered nearby were bound into bundles, attached to the roof, then beaten to create an even finish. Plimoth blacksmiths made rosehead nails to secure the boards on the houses. Plantation carpenters made the clapboards and beams by hand, using authentic seventeenth century tools. The thatched roof houses have wooden chimneys, the kind the original ones had. Furniture has been copied from museum pieces, right down to the gouge marks. Everything is new, recreated. Yet nothing looks too shiny new.

Clay has been packed down, but not perfectly, to make the streets. Not even the guides look particularly fresh-scrubbed. Sometimes their costumes seem almost ragged. But you will discover not all their clothes were black with white collars, the way you learned in elementary schools. Pilgrims enjoyed cheerful clothes, brightened with natural dyes.

Nearby, the Wampanoag Summer Campsite recreates the life the Indians lived at Plymouth before the Pilgrims came. They came to the coast each summer to hunt, fish, and grow crops, including tobacco. Wampanoags in native costume tell about their life here. They demonstrate basket weaving, food preserving, cooking and building.

Close to Plymouth is Duxbury, which one wit called the first suburb. You may visit John Alden's house, now a museum. Pilgrims like Alden, needing land to pasture their cattle, moved to Duxbury.

Thanksgiving time draws tourists to Plymouth like nothing else. Costumed Pilgrims parade through town (there is also a Pilgrim's Progress in August), and there are special dinners. Plimoth Plantation recreates a mid-nineteenth century Victorian Thanksgiving celebration. You have to make reservations a year in advance. Turkey with cornbread stuffing, cranberry sauce, yams, creamed onions, pumpkin pie, and all the food we have come to associate with Thanksgiving are served. Entertainers sing ballads of the period.

More to the point are the authentic seventeenth-century Thanksgiving dinners served all week and with no concession to popular belief. Here you eat like the Pilgrims. Everybody gets a spoon and knife, since nobody used forks back then. Visitors wash in a bowl of water filled with sweet-smelling herbs. The menu includes brown and currant breads, fritters (spinach), oyster soup, carrots, turkey, a lumbardy tart of beets, currants and cheese, and sweet pastries.

No cranberries? No pumpkin pie? Cranberries and pumpkins both could be found here in Pilgrim times, but the earliest records do not show them on the menu. One dish the first settlers learned from the Indians was succotash, made from hulled corn cooked to make a hearty broth. Leftovers fill out the rest. (Succotash and cranberry juice are served without fail at the Pilgrim Society Dinner each Forefather's Day.)

Another good time to visit Plymouth is in late September, when the cranberries are ready for harvest. The Pilgrims landed near the center of cranberry country. The bogs turn a warm cranberry red around harvest time. If anyone needed a reminder of how good a warm cranberry muffin can be, or how tasty cranberry sauce or jelly, the season provides it. Plymouth County has been an important cranberry producing region since the colonial days. A winery that boasts of being "New England's original cranberry winery" is here, housed in a renovated cranberry screening house that dates to 1890.

The Cranberry World Visitors Center, located on the waterfront a ten-minute walk from Plymouth Rock, offers free tours and free cranberry juices. Their exhibits trace the cranberry from colonial times to the present. You can see how cranberries used to be harvested with antique tools, and how they are harvested today at the outdoor working bogs.

The waterfront has always played a central role in Plymouth's economy. In the 1800s, a hundred ships took part in trade and fishing, especially for cod and mackerel. Four ships went whaling. Today, fishing boats still unload their catch daily at Town Wharf. Cod, blues, mackerel, flounder, stripers, and other fish can be caught from the stone jetties. Boats for sport fishing or whale watching are also available. Take-out seafood stands come with picnic tables so visitors can dine on fresh fish while gazing across the waters that the Pilgrims once sailed.

PASTA

Sugar maple taps

Scallops with Broccoli and Noodles

3 cups Wilson Farm Broccoli Flowerets

⅓ lb uncooked medium egg noodles

5 tbsp butter, divided

⅓ cup sliced Wilson Farm Green Onions

½ cup diced Wilson Farm Red Pepper

¾ lb Pier 12 Bay Scallops

3 tbsp sherry

1 tbsp lemon juice

⅓ cup all-purpose flour

1½ cups Shaw's Dairy Milk

1 cup Shaw's Dairy Light Cream

1 tsp salt

⅛ tsp pepper

½ cup shredded Swiss cheese (optional)

- Butter a deep 3 qt casserole dish.
- Wash and steam broccoli until barely tender, about 4 minutes; drain and set aside.
- Cook noodles according to pkg directions until just tender; drain well and set aside.
- Place 2 tbsp butter in large frying pan.
- Preheat oven to 350 degrees.
- Add green onions and pepper; saute 1-2 minutes.
- Add scallops and cook 2-3 minutes.
- Add sherry and lemon juice; cook 1 minute longer.
- Remove from heat and set aside.
- Melt remaining butter in saucepan and stir in flour.
- Blend in milk and cream with wire whisk.
- Cook until sauce boils and thickens.
- Simmer 1 minute; remove from heat.
- Stir in salt and pepper.
- Mix sauce with broccoli mixture including liquid and noodles.
- Add more salt and pepper to taste; spoon into prepared casserole and top with cheese.
- Bake, uncovered, 20-30 minutes, or until sauce is bubbly and cheese melts.
- Serves 6-8.

Pasta with Shiitake Mushrooms and Asparagus

½ lb tagliatelle or other broad egg noodle

1 tbsp butter

1 tbsp olive oil

1 tbsp finely chopped onion

1 lb Delftree Shiitake Mushrooms, sliced

tips from 1 lb asparagus

½ cup chicken broth

salt

3 tbsp dry sherry or Madeira

1 cup Cooper's Hilltop Farm Heavy Cream

1 tsp chopped fresh tarragon
or
½ tsp dried tarragon

salt and freshly ground pepper

- Cook noodles according to pkg directions.

- Heat butter and olive oil in large, deep skillet over medium heat until butter is foamy.

- Add chopped onion and stir 1 minute.

- Add mushrooms and asparagus; toss.

- Add chicken broth, salt lightly and cook partially covered 5-6 minutes, until mushrooms and asparagus are barely cooked.

- Increase heat to high, add sherry or Madeira, cook until most of the liquid has evaporated from pan.

- Add cream and tarragon; cook, shaking pan over heat, until cream thickens slightly and vegetables are tender.

- Season with salt and freshly ground pepper to taste; toss with cooked pasta.

- Serves 4-6.

Chicken Breast Filets and Mushroom Sauce

3-4 qts water

1 tbsp butter

1 (¾ lb) chicken breast, sliced

¼ cup whipping cream (optional)

1 (15.5 oz) jar Trio's Classic Mushroom Sauce

1 (9 oz) pkg Trio's Cracked Black Pepper Fettuccine

2 tbsp grated Parmesan cheese

- Bring water to boil for pasta.
- In non-stick pan, melt butter; cook chicken 1 minute over medium heat.
- Add whipping cream and continue cooking 2 minutes while stirring; set aside.
- In same pan, heat mushroom sauce.
- Return chicken to pan; turn heat off.
- Cook pasta according to pkg directions; drain well and mix with chicken mushroom sauce.
- Sprinkle with Parmesan cheese and serve immediately.
- Serves 2-4.

Turkey Tetrazzini

1 (4 oz) can sliced mushrooms, drained

1 cup diced celery

¼ cup chopped Hibbard Farm Onion

2 tbsp butter

1 tbsp all-purpose flour

1 tsp salt

¼ tsp pepper

1½ cups turkey broth

7 tbsp evaporated milk

1 tbsp Worcestershire sauce

3 cups diced, cooked Twin Willows Turkey

2¼ cups cooked spaghetti

1½ cups shredded Cheddar cheese

¼ cup fine, dry bread crumbs

1 tbsp melted butter

¼ cup grated Parmesan cheese

- Preheat oven to 375 degrees.
- Cook vegetables in butter 20 minutes.
- Stir in flour and seasonings. Cook 3 minutes.
- Add broth, milk and Worcestershire sauce.
- Cook, stirring constantly, until thickened, about 15 minutes.
- Add turkey, spaghetti and cheese.
- Mix bread crumbs with melted butter.
- Sprinkle over turkey mixture in 8" x 8" baking pan.
- Sprinkle Parmesan cheese over crumbs.
- Bake 30 minutes, or until crumbs are lightly browned.
- Serves 6.

Fettuccine Alfredo

3-4 qts water

¾ cup Cains Cholesterol Free Reduced Calorie Mayonnaise

¼ cup skim milk

½ cup grated Parmesan cheese

¼ cup grated Romano cheese

2 cloves garlic, minced

1 tbsp parsley

½ tsp pepper

1 (9 oz) pkg Trio's Garlic & Herbs Fettuccine

- Bring water to rapid boil for pasta.
- In medium saucepan, heat all ingredients except fettuccine, stirring constantly, until smooth.
- Cook fettucine according to pkg directions; drain. Spoon sauce on top.
- Serve immediately.
- Serves 4.

Spinach-Prosciutto Rolls

9 lasagne noodles

2 cups ricotta cheese

1 pkg frozen chopped spinach, thawed and drained well

3 cups shredded Fontina cheese

1 egg, slightly beaten

grated Parmesan or Romano cheese

9 thin slices Carando Prosciutto

½ cup melted butter

- Preheat oven to 375 degrees. Grease 9" x 11" pan.
- Cook lasagne noodles according to pkg directions; drain and pat dry. Set on waxed paper.
- In large bowl, mix ricotta, spinach, Fontina (reserving ½ cup), beaten egg and Parmesan or Romano cheese to taste.
- Spread each lasagne noodle with cheese mixture; lay 1 slice prosciutto lengthwise along each noodle.
- Roll up each noodle and place seam side down in pan.
- Brush each roll with melted butter.
- Cover pan tightly with aluminum foil; bake 45-50 minutes.
- Sprinkle remainder of Fontina cheese on top of each roll and broil 1 minute, or until cheese is melted.
- Serve hot with grated cheese on side.
- Serves 4.

Turkey Lasagne

⅔ cup chopped onion

2 tbsp vegetable oil

1 lb Out Post Farm Ground Turkey

½ tsp salt

⅛ tsp pepper

1½ tsp garlic powder, divided

1 (15.5 oz) can Trio's Light Tomato Sauce

¼ cup chopped green pepper

¼ cup grated Parmesan cheese

½ tsp oregano

2 cups tomato juice

1 (8 oz) pkg lasagne noodles, cooked and drained

¾ cup Hood Country Style Cottage Cheese

¾ cup grated white Cheddar cheese

sliced ripe olives to garnish

- Saute onion in oil. Add turkey, salt, pepper and ½ tsp garlic powder.
- Brown turkey; add tomato sauce, green pepper, Parmesan cheese, oregano, 1 tsp garlic powder and tomato juice.
- Cover; simmer 20 minutes.
- Place ⅓ cooked noodles in bottom of oiled casserole. Cover with ½ turkey sauce.
- Place second layer of noodles over sauce; spread with cottage cheese.
- Cover with remaining noodles and remaining turkey sauce; top with Cheddar cheese.
- Bake at 350 degrees 30-40 minutes.
- Garnish with ripe olives, if desired.
- Serves 6.

Fettuccine Scampi and Broccoli

3 cloves garlic, chopped

crushed hot red pepper to taste

½ cup olive oil

1½ cups Campeche Marisol Shrimp

1 (9 oz) pkg Trio's Egg Fettuccine

1 cup Marini Farm Broccoli Flowerets

3 tbsp sliced fresh chives (optional)

- In non-stick pan saute garlic and crushed red pepper in olive oil.
- When garlic is golden, add shrimp; cook 3 minutes or just until shrimp curl and are firm to the touch.
- Remove pan from heat.
- Cook pasta according to pkg directions. Just before pasta is done, mix in broccoli flowerets.
- Drain pasta and broccoli; don't rinse.
- Toss with scampi sauce in large bowl.
- Garnish with chives and serve immediately.
- Serves 2-4.

Lemon Turkey Primavera

¼ cup butter

*3 cups assorted vegetables (broccoli
flowerets, red pepper strips, sliced
mushrooms, carrot strips, frozen peas,
cauliflower flowerets)*

2 cloves garlic, minced

*1½ cups cooked Twin Willows Turkey,
cut into 1½" x ¼" x ¼" strips*

1 cup Hood Light Cream

2 tbsp capers, drained

1 tsp lemon peel

1 tsp Hartman's Basil

¼ tsp Hartman's Nutmeg

¼ tsp pepper

¼ tsp salt

8 oz dry fettuccine noodles

*1 cup freshly grated Parmesan cheese,
divided*

chopped parsley

- Melt butter in large skillet.
- Add vegetables and garlic; saute until crisp tender, about 5 minutes.
- Add turkey strips; cook 1 minute.
- Stir in cream, capers, lemon peel, basil, nutmeg, pepper and salt.
- Reduce sauce slightly.
- Meanwhile, cook pasta according to pkg directions; rinse and drain well.
- Add hot pasta to skillet with ¾ cup Parmesan cheese.
- Toss gently to combine.
- Serve immediately with additional Parmesan cheese.
- Garnish with chopped parsley.
- Serves 4.

Husband and wife team **Ruth and Milton Bass** write on the following pages about the Berkshires and Pioneer Valley. Ruth is Sunday editor of *The Berkshire Eagle* in Pittsfield, Massachusetts, and has won two all-New England prizes for her weekly column. She's a graduate of Bates College and holds a master's degree in Journalism from Columbia University. An avid cook and gardener, she grew up in the Connecticut River Valley and has lived in the Berkshires for thirty years.

Milton, a native of Berkshire County, is a columnist for *The Berkshire Eagle,* where he was entertainment and travel editor for thirty-five years. He's the author of eleven novels, the most recent of which is *The Belfast Connection.* A member of the Society of American Travel Writers, Milton has written extensively on travel for newspapers and magazines.

PIONEER VALLEY

I t was hardly an original suggestion when Horace Greeley gave his go-west advice. First, he borrowed the phrase from a fellow editorial writer in Indiana. Second, people in Massachusetts had been edging westward for a couple of hundred years.

After all, where else to go when you have landed on the eastern shore of a new land? In the late 1600s, Boston and Salem and New Bedford and Plymouth had reached some level of sophistication, and Western Massachusetts, a mysterious, virgin territory, was out there waiting. So the settlers set forth. What roads and motors have turned into a drive of less than three hours was an adventurous endurance test when horses and feet were the only sources of transportation.

Some came to the fertile plains around the Connecticut River and settled into what's now called the Pioneer Valley, a strip that runs from Vermont to Connecticut in what most Bostonians label Western Massachusetts.

As early as 1636, birthdate of Harvard College in Cambridge, a few families had created a settlement at what is now Springfield, third largest city in the state. From its agricultural beginnings, Springfield moved into manufacturing metal goods and textiles, and became known as "home" of the Springfield rifle.

The U.S. Armory was set up in Springfield by Congress in 1794, and today visitors can see collections of small arms and Civil War muskets at the Springfield Armory National Historical Site.

While the American auto has long been linked to the Midwest, it was in Springfield that one of the first motor car makers, Duryea Motor Wagon Company, began operating in 1895, with one of its cars winning the nation's first auto race that year.

Springfield's connections to the nation at large today rest with more entertainment-oriented things than would have been approved by its prim founders. They were direct descendants of the puritanical coastal settlers who were involved, a little later, with a witch-hunting craze similar to Salem's, albeit less deadly.

That grim aspect belongs strictly to the past. It is here that Milton Bradley, major maker of toys and games, is headquartered; here that the once-famous Indian motorcycles were made, models of which are now housed in a museum; here that basketball began and is commemorated at the Naismith Memorial Basketball Hall of Fame.

While Springfield also has its share of culture—the mid-city, handsome quadrangle of museums encompasses art, science and history—it may be a peach basket from a century ago and a mid-twentieth century ice cream cone that keep it on the wider map.

A man named James Naismith, a professor at Springfield College, invented basketball here in 1891, using a peach basket for a hoop. At the Hall of Fame, such a basket is set up, along with enough colorful tank tops, giant sneakers, statistics and shrines to the greatest stars to sate the desire of the most avid fan.

The ice cream cone was part of a tiny business that two brothers started on Springfield's Main Street. It became Friendly Ice Cream, and the Friendly sign went west as well—and south and north—to become a familiar sight in many states.

Springfield, of course, began with agriculture, and the pattern of its growth, like that of the other communities in the valley, was much influenced by the Connecticut River. The wide meadows along the river have been fertile ground for significant production of onions, cucumbers, potatoes, asparagus, and, unexpectedly for those not brought up here, tobacco.

The Indians first grew tobacco in this valley. And like them, the crops are mostly gone now, although about 200 acres in Massachusetts are still cultivated for shade tobacco, to serve a gourmet market in England.

In the midst of the flat fields of Hadley, Hatfield, Whately and Sunderland, where tobacco plants grew in neat, dark green rows, were the traditional tobacco barns. These were long, weathered rectangles with sides that opened for ventilation once the leaves were hung to dry on cross rafters within.

Most tobacco fields were planted in the open, but some were completely netted in muslin, creating gauzy white patterns across the fields and temperatures of up to 120 degrees inside. While the horse was the traditional pre-tractor work animal in New England, donkeys were often used under the tobacco nets because of their higher tolerance for heat. And workers were sometimes brought in from Jamaica because New Englanders, thick-blooded to withstand winter's cold, suffered as much as their horses in the boiling humidity.

Whether the product was tobacco or onions or milk, farming in the Connecticut Valley was small and family-oriented. When the Poles began to flee Europe in the late 1800s, many of them settled in this valley where they farmed with intense efficiency.

Today there's an annual *kielbasa* festival in the city of Chicopee, a celebration of the spicy Polish sausage that is common fare in area restaurants. Also, cabbage, usually served boiled or raw in cole slaw from a Yankee kitchen, has made new appearances pickled or stuffed with meat.

Each wave of immigration has put its stamp on Western Massachusetts

food, in fact, to the point where New England cooking has become a tough term to define. When Italians were brought in to work the iron mines and marble quarries or do expert masonry and stone work, they gave the tomato and Yankee Doodle's macaroni a whole new life. And the French Canadians, migrating southward to the textile mills that popped up along New England's rivers, brought their own touch to the table. The Greeks came, and so many of them operated restaurants that their ways with food perhaps penetrated the outside world quicker than the others.

It is hard to believe as you drive along the Connecticut River, observing shopping malls, motels, resorts, factories, cities, schools, libraries and thousands of houses, that the agrarian economy here was dominant within the twentieth century.

Fifty, sixty, seventy years ago, it was a farmer's world. Not long after the turn of the century, according to one family's written remembrances, an enterprising young dairy farmer in Greenfield, at the northern end of the Pioneer Valley, was getting up at 3:30 in the morning, doing the chores, milking the cows, bottling the previous night's cooled milk and loading it into his cart.

That work done, he'd have breakfast, head his horse into the village and peddle his milk, retail. Eventually, adding cows and adding customers, he was getting out 170 quarts of milk a day at seven or eight cents a quart, a tidy living in a time when little cash was needed. Noon was the time for the major meal, and by 4:00 in the afternoon, he'd be back in the barn to milk again. Supper would be late and light, and bedtime would be early.

These farmers lived a life in which daylight, weather and the animals' schedules determined what they would do and when they would do it. They had no days off, although many of them were religious enough to do only the necessities—milking the cows, feeding the animals—on Sundays. Nature and necessity governed their lives and probably contributed not only to their self-sufficiency but also to their seeming intolerance of outsiders.

Even in the early twentieth century these people did little socializing.

Colorful Boston

They had no time for it. And they did not use much cash in their daily lives. They were, in fact, almost independent in terms of their food consumption.

People went to the store only occasionally, buying staples like flour and sugar by the barrel. They made their own butter, dried beef to use during the summer when they had little or no refrigeration, used hams they had cured and stored corned beef in crocks in their cellars.

Despite their distance from the sea, these Western Massachusetts farmers ate salt codfish, put up in Gloucester north of Boston in small wooden boxes and so thoroughly salted and dried that it would keep, unrefrigerated, almost indefinitely on the pantry shelf.

In its more modern guise of many machines and much automation, agriculture survives in this riverside strip that runs from the Connecticut border to Vermont, but it has changed. And the land's graduation into more urban ways is no better illustrated than with a look at the growth and change at the University of Massachusetts at Amherst, once a small college town in the midst of the river plain.

Founded in 1863 as Massachusetts Agricultural College because of the area's success with cattle farming, the school had at its core the county extension services, 4-H activities for youth and studies of animal husbandry. But the humanities and sciences kept growing, and while the Stockbridge School of Agriculture is still a vital part of the institution, it has been the University of Massachusetts since the 1940s—a sophisticated school with high-rise dorms, courses and majors of every sort, and students from around the nation.

Just down the way is distinguished Amherst College, named like the town for Lord Jeffrey Amherst, a British general in the French and Indian Wars. In line with the area's puritanical beginnings, Amherst's original charge was to prepare young men for the Protestant ministry in the early nineteenth century, a mission that would seem quite out of place on the present cosmopolitan campus.

Among the austere graduates of days gone by were Henry Ward Beecher, brother of *Uncle Tom's Cabin* author Harriet Beecher Stowe, and President Calvin Coolidge, who lived in nearby Northampton before and after his presidency. Poet Robert Frost was a faculty member for several years.

Amherst and the University of Massachusetts are just two of what's known as the five colleges of the area. Also included are the prestigious women's colleges, Mount Holyoke and Smith, and the newer Hampshire College, all part of the state's rich educational heritage.

The literary atmosphere of Amherst, reflected in the residence of writers like Frost, Helen Hunt Jackson, Eugene Field and Emily Dickinson, is echoed in the unique Jones Library, one of the most elegant of New England's small-town public libraries.

As for Dickinson, her image lives. Reclusive and almost unpublished in life, she is much in view in death, acclaimed as one of the great American poets. Her home, the first brick house in America, is owned by Amherst College and is open to the public by appointment. She is buried in the Amherst Cemetery where, in the 1940s, a group of aspiring young writers from the University of Massachusetts made a habit of visiting her grave in the dark of night, drinking varied beverages and talking to the poet, perhaps seeking some kind of special inspiration.

Amherst is not a town that can forget where its name came from. Facing the lovely green that has managed to remain almost unchanged while the rest of the community has exploded into twentieth century growth, is the Lord Jeffrey Inn, a charming replica of a colonial tavern where documents signed by George Washington, William Pitt, King George II and Lord Jeffrey Amherst are among the displays.

But Amherst as a town was a Johnny-come-lately in the valley. It started out as part of the adjacent town of Hadley and was not settled until 1703, a child compared to its historic neighbor to the north, the town of Deerfield.

If the road were still wagon-wheel rutted and made of dirt instead of asphalt, a person walking now along the shaded main street of Old Deerfield would expect to see women in long, calico dresses and bonnets, wagons and horses, men in wide-brimmed hats.

Now called Historic Deerfield, this mile-long street in Deerfield is a step back in time. But it bears no resemblance to any stereotyped ideas a tourist might have of primitive living in eighteenth or nineteenth century New England. The Asa Stebbins House, built in 1799, is a perfect example. Made from native brick, the substantial structure features Federal-style furniture, a central hallway with a gracefully curving stairway enhanced by a French wallpaper mural of Captain Cook's voyages.

Mantelpieces, cornices, decorated ceilings, an Aubusson rug, a Gilbert Stuart portrait, creamware dishes, fanlighted front door, canopied beds, Federal furniture, English china, early American antiques and Chinese porcelain are overwhelming evidence of success and a life luxuriously lived. All these historic houses are toured in the company of a guide, and no photographs are allowed inside. It's not because they are proprietary about having their collections photographed. It's because, as a guide is likely to explain, "Photographers are always backing up." In these houses, backing up is quite likely to destroy something precious.

Other buildings on what is known as The Street are equally fascinating, and touring takes enough time and energy to make a stop at the Deerfield Inn, rebuilt after a fire several years ago, a welcome intermission.

It is peaceful here in Old Deerfield, especially from the ends of the street where visitors can still see across quiet fields to the foothills of the Berkshires. It is hard to believe that this small place was once filled with fear, the scene of major fires, Indian attacks and massacre.

It was called King Philip's War, named for a Wampanoag Indian chief. Not well-known to many students of American history, the conflict was a bloody business in Massachusetts in the 1670s and Deerfield, the colony's westernmost outpost, was one of the major scenes of combat.

It all came about because of a land dispute between Natick and Dedham, now two densely-populated suburbs of Boston. As the authorities made various land grants, a generous chunk was given to a man named John Eliot for his Christian Indian settlement at Natick.

Apple picking in Harvard

Dedham protested that it already owned that land. In the eventual settlement, the General Court decided in 1663 that Dedham would be given 8,000 acres of land in "any convenient place."

The definition of convenient might have been up for question. The site was Deerfield, considerably north of the thriving settlements at Springfield and Northampton, at the edge of a wilderness that stretched all the way to Montreal.

But John Pyncheon, son of one of Springfield's founders, made the deal with the Pocumtuck Indians in 1667 and bought the 8,000 acres north of Hadley for what was considered an exorbitant price at the time: four pence an acre.

About three years later the first settler arrived. By 1673, twenty families lived in Deerfield, and the house lots on the main street had been laid out pretty much as they still are today. Even when the population reached 125, however, the citizens were apprehensive.

They carried their muskets everywhere, including church. And even as their crops prospered, their worst fears were realized. A band of sixty Pocumtuck Indians attacked, but the settlers ran to their stockades and held them off. Another attack was put down a few days later. But on September 18, 1675, Indians ambushed a group of men convoying a shipment of wheat from Deerfield to Hadley. Only a handful survived a massacre conducted by 700 of King Philip's warriors.

Son of Massasoit, the Wampanoag chief who had signed a treaty with the Pilgrims at Plymouth, King Philip was convinced that his people would be obliterated by the white man. As the whites continued to expand into lands that had been exclusively Indian, he made secret, complex plans for war.

He lost, overpowered eventually by the white man and finally killed by one of his own men. But his impact on Deerfield was to send it back into the wilderness, sixty-four of its men buried in a mass grave and the bereaved settlers drifting southward to pick up their lives again.

Some of the more intrepid, including one John Williams, came back within a few years to rebuild. But in 1704, Indians raided the town again, attacking the Williams house, murdering two of the children and taking the rest captive. Many books, including Williams' own *The Redeemed Captive,* have been written about the dreadful winter trek north to Canada in the hands of the Indians. Williams' wife died during the first part of the march, but the rest, except for a daughter named Eunice, were eventually freed. Eunice was adopted by Christian Indians, married one of them and had three children. The Williams house that stands in Old Deerfield today is of later vintage and is part of the Deerfield Academy campus.

In addition to those in Deerfield, brick houses are not uncommon in the area, many of them made with native brick. Brickmaking was an early industry in Sunderland, a town just north of Amherst where agriculture is still a major industry—from corn and potatoes to blueberries and strawberries. Red sandstone is part of the soil here and a spectacular outcropping called Sugar Loaf provides a chance to drive up and see the valley with its square brown and green fields spread out below.

Modern demands create new ventures in food. Berries are being grown more and more in the valley. In Greenfield, once a town where skilled industry thrived, a major tofu-making business caught on, an incongruity on the surface—but again, just good business sense: All those college students just to the south would be a likely market for such fare in an increasingly vegetarian age.

Here, too, from either side of the valley, visitors can get above it all and see where they are. On the east is Poet's Seat, named in honor of a now-obscure poet who liked to sit up there and do his work. On the west, as the famous Mohawk Trail starts to climb out of the river valley, is a commercially operated tower where somewhat garish signs promise a view of several states. Both offer a chance to see the nearby hills of Vermont, the blue scallops of Mount Tom and Mount Holyoke to the south, the many-hued fields of the remaining rural areas and the town's church steeples.

The same river that made farming such a natural livelihood also created industry. In the eighteenth century, many established towns and cities began to harness their water for power, and both textile and paper mills sprang up throughout Western Massachusetts.

In what is now Chicopee, where the Chicopee River goes through the community and joins the Connecticut, the progression was typical. Blast furnaces were built to process iron ore, then came papermaking, cotton mills, bronze casting—the bronze doors of the Capitol in Washington, D.C., were cast here—cavalry sabres and shotguns. On the lighter side, Chicopee is home to A.G. Spalding, the famous sporting goods manufacturer.

The river still has its hold on what is and isn't done. But the modern use at a place like Northfield, where a giant pumped-storage hydroelectric facility has been constructed, linked environment, recreation and business. And so the visitor may hike, picnic, camp, fish, cross-country ski and snowshoe in the park created by the electric utility. Part of the recreation plan is a ride on the Quinnetukut II, which cruises the Connecticut for one and a half hours, with interpreters discussing history and geology as you float along.

Northfield is known in educational circles for Northfield-Mount Hermon School, once two separate preparatory schools for girls and boys, founded by evangelist Dwight L. Moody. Reflecting Moody's attachment to his native town of Northfield, the schools required that all students do chores about the school and its farm.

Once called Squakheag, the Indian word for "spearing place for salmon," Northfield must have been one of the favorite spots for catching the Atlantic salmon that once heavily populated the Connecticut River. Lost to various dams and industrial installations before environmental concerns gained power, the salmon are a scientific project today, with ladders built to help them run upriver once again.

And like the pioneers who first took on this wilderness that was "west" when they arrived, and the farmers who have persisted despite the competition of giant conglomerates and the pressure of urban development, the salmon seem to be grabbing at each opening, struggling to make it, coming back to the river.

VEGETABLES

Hancock Shaker Village

Cauliflower and Mushrooms with Cheese Sauce

1 head Wilson Orchards Cauliflower

4 tbsp butter, divided

1½ cups thickly sliced mushrooms

3 tbsp all-purpose flour

1½ cups Shady Oaks Farm Milk

½ tsp salt

⅛ tsp pepper

¼ tsp dry mustard

2 cups shredded medium sharp Cheddar cheese

2 tbsp grated Parmesan cheese

- Preheat oven to 375 degrees.
- Butter shallow 1½ qt casserole.
- Break cauliflower into flowerets; wash and cook in boiling, salted water or steam until crisp tender. Drain well.
- Place 1 tbsp butter in frying pan over medium heat.
- Add sliced mushrooms; saute 2-3 minutes, or until soft.
- Set mushrooms aside; make cheese sauce.
- Melt remaining buttter in 3 qt saucepan over medium heat.
- Stir in flour; cook 1 minute, or until smooth.
- Stir in milk and continue to cook, stirring, until mixture thickens and boils.
- Stir in salt, pepper, mustard and Cheddar cheese.
- Cook, stirring, until cheese melts and sauce is smooth; remove from heat.
- Add sauteed mushrooms and cauliflower; stir until well mixed and turn into prepared casserole.
- Sprinkle top with Parmesan cheese.
- Bake 20-30 minutes, or until sauce is bubbly and top is lightly browned.
- Serves 6-8.

Spinach Roma

1½ tbsp butter

2 (10 oz) pkgs frozen, chopped spinach, thawed and well drained

¼ cup grated Parmesan cheese, divided

½ cup chopped Carando Pepperoni

¾ cup ricotta cheese

⅛ tsp garlic powder

1 (8 oz) can tomato sauce

¼ tsp oregano

½ tsp Hartman's Dried Basil

¼ tsp salt

⅛ tsp pepper

1 tbsp grated Romano cheese

- Preheat oven to 350 degrees.
- In large frying pan, melt butter over low heat.
- Add spinach, 1 tbsp Parmesan cheese and next 8 ingredients; stir well.
- Cook 5 minutes, or until spinach is done.
- Spoon into 9″ pie plate that has been sprayed with non-stick cooking spray.
- Smooth top of mixture; sprinkle additional Parmesan cheese in lattice pattern on top.
- Bake 30 minutes. Let stand 10 minutes before serving.
- Serves 8.

Broiled Tomatoes with Dill Sour Cream Sauce

½ cup Czepiel's Sour Cream or Nonfat Yogurt

¼ cup Cains All Natural Mayonnaise

2 tbsp chopped onion

¼ tsp dried dillweed

¼ tsp salt

4 large Volante Farm Tomatoes

salt and pepper

butter

- Mix first 5 ingredients and chill.
- Core tomatoes and cut in half crosswise.
- Season cut surface with salt and pepper; dot with butter.
- Grill over medium fire 5 minutes; spoon sauce on tomatoes and serve at once.
- Serves 6-8.

Grilled Tomatoes

4 Gove Farm Tomatoes

½ cup finely crushed State Line
Potato Chips

2 tbsp minced parsley

1 tbsp minced onion

dash cayenne

1 tbsp butter

- Cut tomatoes in half and set aside.
- Combine potato chips, parsley, onion, cayenne and butter.
- Use fingers or pastry blender to mix and crumble together thoroughly.
- Sprinkle generously over tomato halves and place on grill to cook, 3-5 minutes.
- Serves 6-8.

Fresh Creamed Corn

2 tbsp butter

½ cup chopped onion

½ cup chopped red bell pepper

½ cup chopped green bell pepper

1 clove garlic, minced

3 cups fresh Wilson Farm Corn Kernels

¼ cup chopped green onion

1 cup Hood Half & Half

2 tbsp chopped fresh basil

2 tsp chopped fresh thyme

salt and pepper

1 tbsp all-purpose flour

4 slices Blood Farm Bacon, cooked,
drained and crumbled

1 tbsp fresh parsley

- Melt butter in large skillet.
- Saute onion, peppers and garlic until tender, about 3 minutes.
- Add corn, green onion, cream, basil and thyme.
- Simmer, uncovered, 5 minutes, or until corn is just tender.
- Season to taste with salt and pepper.
- Sprinkle flour over corn mixture.
- Cook and stir until thickened, about 2 minutes.
- Sprinkle with bacon and parsley.
- Serve immediately.
- Serves 4-6.

Corn Oysters

2 cups tightly packed, fresh cooked
Marini Farm Sweet Corn

3 Johnson Poultry Farm Eggs,
separated

¼ cup plus 1 tbsp all-purpose flour

½ tsp baking powder

1 tbsp sugar

1½ tbsp melted butter

1 tsp salt

¼ tsp pepper

- Place corn in large bowl.
- Add 3 egg yolks; stir until blended.
- Sift dry ingredients. Add to corn mixture; stir until blended.
- Add melted butter, salt and pepper; thoroughly blend.
- Beat egg whites until stiff peaks form.
- Fold whites into corn mixture.
- Drop by teaspoonfuls onto hot, oiled griddle.
- Fry until browned on both sides, turning once.
- Serves 8-10.

Sauteed Shiitake Mushrooms

4 tbsp olive oil

caps from 1½ lbs Delftree Shiitake
Mushrooms, thinly sliced

2 cloves garlic, finely chopped

2 tbsp finely chopped parsley

1 tsp fresh thyme leaves
or
½ tsp dried thyme

½ tsp chopped fresh rosemary leaves or
½ tsp crumbled dried rosemary

¼ cup Chicama Vineyards Chardonnay

½ cup tomato puree or tomato sauce

salt and freshly ground pepper

- Heat oil in large skillet over medium heat.
- Add mushrooms, garlic and herbs.
- Cook slowly, partially covered, stirring occasionally, until mushrooms have softened, about 10 minutes.
- Add wine, tomato puree or tomato sauce; stir.
- Simmer, uncovered, 10 minutes longer, until liquid has thickened.
- Season with salt and pepper.
- Serves 6.

Broccoli with Sour Cream and Cashews

*1 large head Arena Farms Broccoli,
washed and cut into flowerets*

1 cup water

½ tsp salt

1 cup Czepiel's Sour Cream

4 oz sharp American cheese, grated

½ tsp grated lemon peel

1 tbsp lemon juice

¼ tsp salt

dash white pepper

3 oz salted cashews, chopped

- Steam broccoli 5-6 minutes in boiling salted water.
- Place broccoli in shallow ovenproof serving dish; keep warm.
- Heat broiler.
- Combine remaining ingredients, except cashews; spoon over broccoli.
- Sprinkle nuts over all.
- Place under broiler until heated thoroughly, taking care not to burn cashews.
- Serve immediately.
- Serves 6.

Ratatouille

⅓ cup La Spagnola Canola Oil

2 small onions, thinly sliced

2 small green peppers, thinly sliced

1-2 cloves garlic, minced

*1 medium eggplant, unpeeled
and chopped*

*2 medium Idylwilde Farm Zucchini,
unpeeled and thinly sliced*

2 Volante Farm Tomatoes, thinly sliced

salt and oregano

- Heat oil in large skillet.
- Saute onions and green peppers with garlic over low heat until vegetables are limp.
- Remove from pan and set aside.
- Add eggplant and zucchini to pan; saute and keep turning until slightly softened.
- Add tomatoes, salt, oregano, onions and green peppers; cover and simmer 30 minutes, stirring occasionally.
- Serves 4-6.

Zucchini Provencale

2 tbsp olive oil

2 cloves garlic, minced

1-2 medium Verrill Farm Zucchini, sliced into 1/2" rounds

3-4 tomatoes, cut into eighths

1/2 tsp salt

1 tsp basil

1 bay leaf

4-6 slices Baldwin Hill Bread, toasted

1 cup grated Parmesan cheese

- Preheat oven to 350 degrees.
- In large skillet, heat oil; add garlic, zucchini and tomatoes. Cook 5 minutes.
- Add salt and herbs; cook 25-30 minutes.
- Lightly oil 6" x 10" casserole.
- Spoon layer of sauce into bottom of dish; add layer of bread slices. Sprinkle with cheese.
- Repeat and sprinkle cheese on top.
- Cover with foil; bake 25 minutes.
- Uncover and bake another 5 minutes.
- Serves 4-6.

Zucchini Stir-Fry

1-2 tbsp olive oil

3 cloves garlic, minced

1 large onion, chopped

1/2 cup The Herb Garden Chive Flower Wine Vinegar

2 cups stewed tomatoes

1 tbsp steak sauce

3 small Clegg Farm Zucchini, sliced

1 tsp Hartman's Dried Basil

1/2 tsp Hartman's Oregano

1/2 tsp Hartman's Thyme

3 cups cooked rice

grated Parmesan cheese

- Add olive oil to skillet; saute garlic and onion until translucent.
- Add vinegar, tomatoes and zucchini; stir well.
- Cover and simmer over low heat 15 minutes; add herbs. Cover and simmer another 15 minutes.
- Sprinkle with cheese; serve as side dish or over rice.
- Serves 4-6.

Baked Stuffed Squash

2, 8" Spence Farm Summer Squashes
or Zucchini

1 cup bread crumbs

½ cup grated Parmesan or
Cheddar cheese

2 tbsp chopped onion

¼ tsp Mrs. G's Herb Salt

- Boil whole squash 10 minutes. Immerse in cold water.
- Remove ends and slice lengthwise.
- Scoop out pulp, being careful not to tear shells.
- Mix pulp with bread crumbs, cheese, onion and garlic salt.
- Stuff shells with mixture and place in baking dish with ⅛" water.
- Bake at 350 degrees 15 minutes.
- Serves 4-6.

Squash Apple Casserole

4 tbsp butter, divided

¼ cup brown sugar

1 tsp cinnamon

½ cup coarsely chopped walnuts, pecans
or chestnuts (optional)

salt

2½ cups Arena Farms Squash or
Pumpkin, cut into 1" chunks

1½ cups pared and sliced Carlson
Orchards Apples

- Melt 3 tbsp butter; combine with brown sugar, cinnamon, nuts and salt.
- Place layer of squash or pumpkin in 2 qt casserole dish; drizzle with butter and sugar mixture.
- Top with layer of apples; drizzle with mixture.
- Repeat until all ingredients are used.
- Dot with remaining butter.
- Cover; bake in 350 degree oven 45 minutes-1 hour, or until both apples and squash are tender.
- Serves 4.

Leeks and Cider

6-8 leeks, 1½" thick
3 tbsp butter
¾-1 cup West County Hard Cider
½ cup water

- Wash leeks carefully and trim tops.
- Cut remaining white "roots" into rounds of elongated slices.
- Rinse with cold water.
- Heat heavy pan; cool slightly before adding butter.
- Melt, but don't brown or burn butter.
- Saute leeks until slightly tender.
- Add enough cider to cover bottom of pan.
- Cover and simmer until done, about 10 minutes.
- Remove leeks to platter and keep warm; simmer and stir cider until almost caramelized, 5 minutes or less. Do not burn.
- Pour over leeks and serve immediately.
- Serves 6.

Mushroom Tempura

¾ cup cornstarch
¼ cup all-purpose flour
1 tsp baking powder
½ tsp salt
¼ tsp pepper
1 Westminster Farm Egg, slightly beaten
½ cup water
La Spagnola Corn Oil
¼ lb Delftree Shiitake Mushrooms

- Mix dry ingredients; add egg and water and mix again.
- Heat ¼" corn oil in skillet for frying.
- Dip mushrooms in batter and fry until golden brown.
- Drain on paper towel and serve.
- Serves 2.

Potatoes Romano

6 large Tater Delight Potatoes, cooked
and cubed

2 onions, chopped

2 cups Czepiel's Cottage Cheese

1 cup Czepiel's Sour Cream

1 cup cubed Blood Farm Ham

1 cup fresh or frozen peas, cooked

1 cup shredded Cheddar cheese

paprika

- Combine potatoes and onions; stir in cottage cheese and sour cream.
- Add ham and peas.
- Pour into buttered 2½ qt casserole.
- Sprinkle with Cheddar cheese and paprika.
- Bake at 350 degrees 30 minutes.
- Serves 6-8.

Stuffed Potatoes

8 baking Tater Delight Potatoes

½ cup butter

1 cup Czepiel's Sour Cream

½ tsp Mrs. G's Herb Pepper

1 Johnson Poultry Farm Egg, beaten

1 cup grated Cheddar cheese

1 tbsp chives

1 tbsp Mrs. G's Herb Salt

paprika

8 slices Outlook Farm Bacon, fried
crisp and crumbled

- Bake potatoes 1 hour at 400 degrees.
- Cut in half lengthwise and scoop out potatoes, leaving shells.
- Combine all ingredients except bacon; mash until creamy.
- Stir in bacon.
- Stuff back into potato skins.
- Freeze if not ready to use.
- When ready to serve, thaw and/or heat in oven at 350 degrees 30 minutes, or until thoroughly heated.
- Serves 12-16.

Dilled Baby Carrots

18 baby carrots

3 tbsp Chicama Vineyards White
Wine Vinegar

2 tsp Hartman's Dillweed

- Place small carrots in steamer or double boiler; cook until crisp tender.
- Place in serving bowl; add vinegar and dillweed. Toss until completely covered with dillweed.
- Serve warm or chilled.
- Serves 3-4.

THE BERKSHIRES

Ask longtime residents of Great
Barrington, North Adams,
Lenox, Williamstown or Pittsfield where they live, and the answers are
likely to be the same: Berkshire County.

Few in Boston, Hyannis or Pelham would announce themselves as
denizens of Suffolk, Barnstable or Hampshire counties, respectively.
But in the Berkshires, while county is unimportant governmentally, it is
paramount geographically.

It's always been that way. Nor was it any accident that the English
settlers' urge to go west paused in this broad valley of the Connecticut
River. To the west was the rugged Hoosac Range, and for some years it
formed a barrier that the colonists did not breach.

Eventually, of course, they went over it. But before that, the Dutch
reversed colonization's general movement and moved east from the
Hudson River settlements, and Connecticut colonists pushed north
through the valley of the Housatonic River.

So Dutch farmers moving east were credited with creating the first Berkshire County settlement in 1692 in what is now Mount Washington, many years after Deerfield had already built a substantial chunk of its history. Known nationally today as one of the first places in the nation to record its vote in presidential elections, Mount Washington also holds the title of smallest town in Massachusetts.

Some settlers from eastern Massachusetts followed after the Dutch had made their forays, but nearly all of them came across at the southern end of the county where the hills were lower. They moved into what was known as Lower Housatonnic Township, now Sheffield, a town incorporated in 1733.

More than 150 years later, during the nation's vibrant economic expansion, railroad developers actually had to make their way through the mountains of Berkshire County. It took twenty-four years, 195 lives and $20 million to build the 25,000-foot Hoosac Tunnel so the railroad could reach North Adams. That was in 1875. The Mohawk Trail, now a familiar and famous state highway from Williamstown to Greenfield, wasn't completed until 1914.

Even today, although the Berkshires are favored by visitors from all over the world, sprinkled with condominiums and loved by second-home owners, the region is still in many ways as separate from the rest of Massachusetts as it was in the seventeenth century. Berkshirites are likely to fuss mightily about home rule, which means they want the state to leave them alone, and complain the next day that the legislators at the State House in Boston have forgotten them and they might as well secede and become part of adjoining New York State.

Maybe it's the changeable weather that makes them so contrary. Killing frosts are supposed to be gone by mid-May but may capriciously strike the first week in June and, in the valleys, paint deathly white patches early in September. Nor'casters blow, hurricanes threaten, and thunderstorms are likely to circle around for a second hit after they gave every sign of leaving. Snowstorms can be as soft as a Christmas card scene or howling wild.

Despite all that, few days anywhere are more lovely than a perfect one in Berkshire County. In winter that means crisp air, bright blue sky, snow on the ground, February sun. In spring—which sometimes escapes into summer without really occurring at all—it means a warm day in May or June with puffy white clouds, a light breeze. In summer, it's hot days with low humidity, dropping into cool, breezy evenings in August when a sweater is essential. In fall, it's Amherst author Helen Hunt Jackson's *October's Bright Blue Weather*.

Millions of years ago, this landscape was probably not nearly as interesting. Upheavals of land followed by glacial scraping and cutting and carving made valleys, lakes, rivers. And now, the mountains left by that moving wall of ice, mere bumps in terms of New York's Adirondacks and a virtual plain compared to the towering Rockies, have continued to maintain Berkshire's guard against incursions from the east.

At the top of it all is Mount Greylock, highest point in the state at 3,491 feet, which offers some of the best of the area's recreation in the wild: camping, cross-country skiing, hiking, nature activities, sightseeing, even downhill skiing for the adventurous few who first climb the lift-less mountain on their skis and then shoot down the venerable, but aptly named Thunderbolt Trail.

The county's space runs roughly from eastern hilltop to the New York State border, also pretty much a mountain ridgeline, and from the Vermont border to Connecticut. Virtually equidistant from New York and Boston, its loyalties have long been split between the two major cities.

Summer music at the famous festival at Tanglewood is provided by the Boston Symphony Orchestra. But the audience, in part because the north/south roads were streamlined first, is heavily weighted toward New Yorkers. When the Massachusetts Turnpike was built, years after New York's interstate and the Taconic Parkway, Bostonians learned slowly that they could reach the Berkshires in less than three hours. New Yorkers had been enjoying the area for years.

In the still sparsely populated towns along the mountaintops, appropriately dubbed hilltowns, summer residents and commuters live alongside potato farmers, blueberry growers, Christmas tree farmers.

Like the Connecticut Valley, this area began with farming and, in fact, was home of the first agricultural fair. That bucolic affair was organized by one Elkanah Watson and his Berkshire Agricultural Society in 1810. It was held on Park Square, the central common nearly always found at the heart of New England towns. This one has a difference that may suggest the independence of the area: Park Square is oval.

Given their late start, the Berkshires ran fast to catch up with the earlier settled areas. And thus, in 1774, a county convention endorsed one of the first boycotts when it urged "non-consumption of British manufactures." Less than two months later, in an episode rarely taught in American Revolutionary history, 1,500 unarmed men seized the courthouse in the town of Great Barrington and blocked royal judges from the bench. This event, shots heard round the world and tea parties notwithstanding, has been termed "first open resistance to British rule in America." In that same year, two regiments of Berkshire Minute Men were organized.

And when the Revolution was over, its heroes were remembered forever with the renaming of seven Berkshire towns: Otis, Lee, Hancock, Mount Washington, Washington, Adams and North Adams.

Eventually, of course, investors came to harvest the area's natural resources and harness the power of the Housatonic River. Berkshire marble quarries supplied marble for the Capitol at Washington, D.C., and in a small mill in Lee, thousands of headstones were cut for the graves of soldiers buried in Arlington (Va.) Cemetery.

Along the river, paper mills sprang up, including the famous Crane Paper Co., which was founded in Dalton by 24-year-old Zenas Crane in 1801. It's still going strong and continues to manufacture not only premium papers but also the only paper on which the U.S. currency has been printed for decades. A number of major paper mills remain, but the textile mills that also sprang up along the river are long gone, vanished south in search of cheaper labor and lower fuel costs.

While thousands think of the area as primarily a giant resort, there's business in these hills. Farming continues, in small quantity and concentrated more on fruits and vegetables than on dairy products. A few farmers in Richmond, Lanesboro, Hancock, Lee and Cummington, still harvest sap each spring and boil it down to the amber maple syrup for which New England is famous. But many Berkshirites these days work in industry or in offices. Open spaces are shrinking, and in several of the communities, land trusts have been incorporated to protect the still undeveloped areas, the mountain tops and the purity of the water. The inhabitants realize the uniqueness of Berkshire County and are going all out to preserve it, just as they have, in recent years, polished up the area's Victorian houses and restored them to their turn-of-the-century majesty.

Despite the hardship of its beginnings, when farmers were fighting the rocky soil, Berkshire County did not take long to start on its road to present-day tourism.

The castle-like mansions of Newport, Rhode Island, are perhaps the best-known of New England's summer retreats for the rich. But Lenox, in the heart of Berkshire County, had the greatest number of what were known as its "cottages," grand houses of the very rich, built from about 1880 until World War I changed the American way of life.

At the turn of the century, the county had seventy-five such estates, the largest being the Anson Phelps Stokes place called Shadowbrook, which had one hundred rooms. Bellefontaine elegantly reflected the Petit Trianon in France, and today's Berkshire tourist can still see it, preserved at the core of a full-fledged, very twentieth century spa called Canyon Ranch. Other buildings remain from the era of elegance, some of them handsomely used today. Blantyre and Wheatleigh, for instance, the former built by a turpentine magnate, the latter by a banker, are beautifully kept and among the Berkshires most expensive hostelries.

Among the luminaries of the so-called Gilded Age was author Edith Wharton, who wrote her famous *House of Mirth* at her home, The Mount, in Lenox. Patrician and exacting, she had a reputation for looking down on the natives. She owned the first car that drove to the top of Mount Greylock, frequently entertained Henry James at her home and buried her dogs, who all had French names, on a little knoll at her estate, each plot marked with a headstone.

The Mount was purchased in 1980 by the National Trust for Historic Preservation, which is working to bring it back to its original splendor. Tours are conducted in the summer and fall. The Mount also serves as the headquarters for Shakespeare & Company, which each year presents playlets in the house. The company also performs one Shakespeare play each summer on stages built on the spacious lawns.

Although two famous architects worked on the design of Wharton's mansion, she put her stamp on everything, insisting that window for window and door for door, it be symmetrical, even to the point of false windows and fake doors.

She had a water-powered elevator, twelve household servants, gardeners and a chauffeur. As she "whizzed" past the farmers in the Berkshire towns, she noticed Plainfield, which became the background for her novel *Ethan Frome.* The story's plot was based on an actual accident that occurred in Lenox.

Probably unperturbed by Wharton's disdain, the natives were secure in their pride in being what's known as "borners;" the newcomer label stays put for years in these small towns.

Wharton, after all, was not the Berkshires' first brush with culture, nor its last. Writers, poets and artists were attracted to the charms of the county almost from its beginnings. At first they came to commune with nature and then as their numbers grew, they came to commune with each other.

One of the most notable communions occurred on Sept. 4, 1850, when a 31-year-old New York writer named Herman Melville bought a 160-acre farm near the city of Pittsfield where he hoped to combine his literary efforts with the tilling of the soil.

On his first plowing of the fields, he dug up an Indian arrowhead, probably Mohican, and so he named his property Arrowhead.

After several years at sea, some of it on whalers, the young Melville had written two books, *Typee* and *Omoo,* about his South Sea adventures, including his capture by natives and subsequent escape. From these he gained some reputation and just enough money on which to get by. His subsequent three books didn't do too well, and he hoped that by moving to the countryside he would rekindle his creative fire. He brought with him the unfinished manuscript of his current piece of work, which he had tentatively titled *Moby Dick*.

Melville knew the area well. He had spent boyhood summers on the adjoining estate of his uncle, Major Thomas Melville, and had grown to love the Berkshires for its beauty and serenity. He hoped the tranquil atmosphere would allow his imagination to roam the wild seas he was attempting to recreate.

The uniqueness of the house, which is now owned by the Berkshire Historical Society and open for tours, lay in its gigantic chimney, which Melville described in detail in an article in *Putnam's* magazine. The writer and his wife waged a continual battle over the chimney. She wanted it torn down to make room for a grand entrance hall. He wanted it exactly as it was.

He did agree to discuss the matter with an expert, one Hiram Scribe, and this is Melville's recounting of the meeting:

> "'The root of the matter,' said Hiram Scribe. 'This
> is a most remarkable structure, Sir.'
> 'Yes,' said I (Melville) complacently.
> 'But large as it appears above the roof, I would not
> have inferred the magnitude of this foundation,
> Sir,' eyeing it critically.
> Then taking out his rule, he measured it.
> 'Twelve feet square; one hundred and forty-four
> square feet! Sir, this house would appear to have been
> built simply for the accommodation of your chimney.'
> 'Yes, my chimney and me. Tell me candidly now,' I
> added. 'Would you have such a chimney abolished?'
> 'I wouldn't have it in a house of mine, sir, for a gift,'
> was the reply. 'It's a losing affair altogether, sir'."

Luckily for posterity, Melville won out, and today we can inspect the gigantic chimney with quotations from his stories painted on its hearth, and imagine him sitting in his warm corner puffing away on his ever-present clay pipe.

Although he was living in the countryside, Melville's thoughts were never far from the sea, and from his writing room on the second floor of the north side of the house, he had a clear view of Mount Greylock, twenty miles or so to the north. To Melville the double-humped mountain looked like a "sperm whale breaching," and thus the shape of his novel also changed.

It wasn't only Greylock that reshaped Melville's thinking. It was a picnic. Oliver Wendell Holmes, the Boston doctor and poet who spent his summers in Pittsfield, invited Melville to go on a picnic with several other friends, including Nathaniel Hawthorne, who was then living in the adjacent town of Lenox.

The picnic was set for Monument Mountain in Great Barrington, from whose craggy top, Indian legend had it, a love-distraught young maiden had hurled herself to her death on the rocks below. William Cullen Bryant, who was born in the town of Cummington and practiced law in Great Barrington for several years, has immortalized the mountain in several of his poems. When the party of seven reached the top, Holmes broke out a bottle of champagne, and toasts were exchanged.

But one of those sudden Berkshire thunderstorms sent everyone scurrying for cover, and Melville and Hawthorne went under the protection of a large rock where they held serious discussion for a long period.

The friendship became quite intense in the following few months with Hawthorne finishing up *The House of the Seven Gables,* and Melville working with renewed vigor on *Moby Dick.* Hawthorne wrote a letter to his family in which he stated that "On the hither side of Pittsfield sits Herman Melville, shaping out the gigantic conception of his white whale, while the gigantic shape of Greylock looms upon him from his study window."

Melville wrote four other novels in his thirteen years in Pittsfield, but none was successful, and finally he moved his family back to New York where he spent the rest of his life in obscurity, never knowing that his white whale had gained immortality.

A broad open field preserves the view of Greylock from Melville's writing table, and Hawthorne's tiny house across the road from Tanglewood in Lenox exists in a reproduction. You cannot see the house where Henry Wadsworth Longfellow wrote the poem "The Clock on the Stairs" because it is now the site of Pittsfield High School.

Whereas both Melville and Hawthorne were moody, brooding men, Oliver Wendell Holmes was both brash and witty. His most famous Berkshire poem, titled "The Deacon's Masterpiece," started out by asking:

"Have you heard of the wonderful one-hoss shay,
That was built in such a logical way
It ran a hundred years to a day?"

The poem tells about the deacon's search for perfection for his carriage by using materials that would never deteriorate. However, as with everything else, nothing lasts forever, and on a hundred years to the day the wagon disappeared into dust. The last two lines are:

"End of the wonderful one-hoss shay.
Logic is logic. That's all I say."

Holmes's own one-hoss shay is now in the possession of the Berkshire Museum, which indicates that a carriage can last for more than a hundred years. The museum has many other fine exhibits, especially from American artists of the nineteenth century, and it also recently installed a small aquarium that compactly takes visitors to Pacific and Atlantic reefs and to the Housatonic River. One other inhabitant is a nine-year-old Texas Armadillo named Amy who used to follow science curator Thom Smith around the halls until he created her a special space of her own.

Writers still find the Berkshires a stimulating place. Pulitzer Prize-winning poet laureate Richard Wilbur writes his verse and tends his vegetable garden in the town of Cummington. Foreign correspondent-historian William L. Shirer, whose *Rise and Fall of the Third Reich* became an American classic, works diligently away in his Lenox house, as busy as ever in his mid-eighties. And playwright William Gibson, who wrote the prize-winning play about Helen Keller, *Miracle Worker,* still spends each working day in the little cabin he built behind his house in Stockbridge.

With two top echelon regional theaters in the county in summer, well-known actors and playwrights are frequently working in this area. And because the Berkshires are only two and a half hours from New York, scores of TV and film writers and television executives come here to play and escape the pressures of the city.

One of the ways they escape is to eat. With the exception of the Shakers, no particular group has spiced the county's food offerings more than any other. Yet, perhaps because in winter there's not a lot of things to do, perhaps because ingredients are ripe and fresh and good, Berkshire County has a long menu of varied good, and sometimes excellent, restaurants.

These dining places are of a special calibre because of the standards set by a giant of a lady who stood only four feet, ten inches tall. Her name was Mrs. Henrietta Grosso (Kate to her friends, Mama to the general public), and in 1929 she decided to open a small roadside stand on Route 7 in the town of New Ashford to supplement the income from her equally small meat and grocery store in the town of North Adams.

The beginning menu was classic American—hotdogs and hamburgers—but she quickly added spaghetti with her own special tomato sauce, and within a few years she introduced specialties that made everybody in Berkshire County beat a dinner path to her door. She named a new and bigger restaurant The Springs because it was situated near a natural spring.

"I always insist that everything be the freshest," she told an interviewer in 1964. "We didn't have any refrigeration in the early days, and I got in the habit of going to the market every day. Now I know it's still the best thing to do."

As the restaurant prospered and her three children pitched in to help,

Mrs. Grosso started the custom of visiting New York seven times a year for a four-day stay each time. "That's all you can take in that city," she said. "Four days on the nose."

But while she was in the city, she was eating both lunch and dinner at the finest restaurants, and she almost always ended up talking to the owner and chef and inspecting the kitchen. Each time she returned to New Ashford a new dish or other nicety would be added to the restaurant and its ambience. Several of the most prominent chefs in the Berkshires started as vegetable choppers at The Springs, worked their way up the ladder, and eventually opened their own restaurants.

Mrs. Grosso died many years ago, but The Springs still flourishes, run by her son and grandson. And time has caught up with Mama Grosso's attitude on vegetables and fruits. Organic farm operations have sprung up around the county, and farmers' roadside stands, some still with a can of money and an honor system, are flourishing.

In Williamstown, Caretaker Farm takes pride in its exclusion of chemicals for either fertilizer or pesticides. In South County, Taft Farm and a rapidly growing organic gardening cooperative can hardly keep up with the demand from year-rounders who don't bother to garden and second-homers who are tired of wilted city lettuce and wax-coated cucumbers.

In addition, as Massachusetts officially campaigns to have more food raised within the boundaries of the relatively small and urban state, Berkshire's visitors have their favorite farm stands where they regularly stop for whatever's in season. One small place may have only asparagus and the fragile raspberries, the next opens only in August for sweet corn, fresh and living up to its name. Apples are a major crop, and growers like Bartlett's in Richmond and Jaeschke's in Adams pick thousands of bushels of several different varieties in the crisp weather of September and October. At Bartlett's roadside outlet, cider without any preservatives is made behind a huge glass window so visitors can watch.

The Shaker influence on food had its roots in 1770 when Ann Lee, a leader of a religious group that called itself the United Society of

Believers in Christ's Second Coming, responded to a vision that instructed her to become "Mother of the New Creation," and to form a new community in New England. Bringing a core group, she settled in 1776 in what is now Watervliet, a small community near Albany, New York.

Music was an integral part of Shaker religious services, and as the members danced, they bobbed and weaved while circling the meeting room, and thus became known as the Shaking Quakers and finally just Shakers. In time, they established eighteen communities in nine different states.

In 1790, one of these communities took root in Hancock, the town immediately west of Pittsfield, some thirty-four miles from the original New York State locale. In 1792, another community was settled in the nearby town of Tyringham. Since they were excellent farmers and quite inventive, the Shakers produced not only food for themselves, but enough to ship to many areas of the country.

Herbs were a specialty, especially those used in medicinal preparations, which were sold not only in this country but also in London, Paris and Bombay, India. The Shaker herb catalogue in 1864 listed 354 kinds of medicinal plants, barks, roots, seeds and flowers, plus as many extracts, powders, elixirs and ointments. Although they had withdrawn from "The World," the world was still much with them, and they prospered by divining and serving its needs.

They made brooms, were the first to put vegetable seeds in little packets to sell, created furniture and developed an architecture that was functional and beautiful.

Because of their rule of celibacy and because the world changed much in the middle of the nineteenth century, the ranks of the Shakers began to diminish, which meant that community after community began to close down. In 1959, there were only three sisters left from the high point of 300 members at the Hancock commune, and developers were after the land. A group of thirty local people formed an organization to preserve the eighteen structures as a living museum, and today several thousand people visit each year to learn about Shaker life and arts.

Because the Shakers believed everything they did was done for God, they were consistent in wanting everything beautiful as well as simple and utilitarian. The food they grew and cooked was as healthy as it was tasty. They even experimented with vegetarianism for a ten-year period. The diet was rich in that butter, milk and cream were plentiful, but it was also subtle in many ways because of their prodigious use of the herbs they grew.

At periodic intervals they would give what they called "World Peoples' Dinners" to which outsiders were invited, hoping to attract new converts. The Hancock Shaker Village, which drew 72,000 visitors last year, now presents "An Evening at Hancock Shaker Village" each Saturday night during the summer season. This includes a candlelight dinner of Shaker food plus a tour of the buildings. The dinner might include Eldress Clymena's Tomato Soup, Brother Ricardo's Favorite Chicken Pudding, Sister Lettie's Veal Loaf, Sister Abigail's Blue Flower (of the chive plant) Omelet, Sister Mary's Zesty Carrots, Agreeable Onions, Sister Olive Wheeler's Diet Bread, Sister Hattie's Huckleberry Muffins, Sister Emma Neal's Rule for Soft Gingerbread, Mary Whicher's Orange Sponge Custard and Shaker Gingerade.

Touring the twenty buildings, including the unique Round Barn, and watching the craftsmen make tin dustpans, a Shaker invention, observing the chair maker, the blacksmith, the hat maker can bring on quite an appetite. The original Shakers ate their meals in fifteen minutes or less before getting back to work. It's much more satisfying to do it this more leisurely way.

One of the best pies in Berkshire County is delightful to look at but not to eat. It's called the Sedgwick Pie, and it is situated in the Stockbridge Town Cemetery.

The "pie" was started when the Honorable Judge Theodore Sedgwick, who practiced law in the towns of Great Barrington and Sheffield and served in both the United States House of Representatives and Senate, died in 1813. He was buried in the center of the family plot in Stockbridge next to the grave of his wife, Pamela, who had pre-deceased him by six years. An obelisk was placed over the site, and a privet hedge planted around them.

Nobody knows exactly what the plan was to begin with, but all succeeding generations of Sedgwicks, including some of their dogs, have been buried in circles around the founding pair. In the first circle is a former slave named Mumbet who had served the family faithfully for nearly fifty years. Mumbet had belonged to a Col. John Ashley. Mumbet reportedly had run away when allegedly hit on the arm with a kitchen shovel. She gained refuge with the Sedgwicks, and when Col. Ashley brought suit to have his "property" returned, Judge Sedgwick represented Mumbet and won her freedom.

In a previous case, Judge Sedgwick had ruled that the law of nature should be the law of the land, and that no person could hold property in the person of another. Thus, in Berkshire County, the fight against slavery began nearly one hundred years before the Civil War.

The Sedgwick family has distinguished itself in literature, the church, government service and journalism, but no matter where in the world they might live, they are brought back to Stockbridge for burial in the "pie." The tradition is to have the casket moved from the church in Stockbridge to the burial plot in a horse and wagon, both draped in black, and members of the family following behind for the half-mile distance.

In 1970, Gen. William R. Bond was killed by a sniper in Vietnam, and the Army sent seventy Green Berets to march in his cortege. The horse became too frisky as the procession started, so he was unyoked, and the general's nephews pulled the wagon to the cemetery.

Tourists find a thousand things to do in Berkshire County, from picnicking to looking at the miniature Lincoln Memorials in sculptor Daniel Chester French's studio to visiting public gardens and old houses to climbing up the mountaintops. But the three things they want to do most, the experts say, are attend a concert at Tanglewood, have a drink on the porch at the Red Lion Inn in Stockbridge and visit the Norman Rockwell museum. Those are all great things to do, but you just might have a piece of the "Pie" as well.

DESSERTS

Sunrise at Sunderland, Pioneer Valley

Apple Cobbler with Cider Syrup

Short Dough:

¼ cup shortening

2 tbsp sugar

¼ tsp salt

1 egg

1 tbsp lemon juice

1 cup Green Friedman
All-Purpose Flour

2 tsp baking powder

2 tbsp milk

Filling:

5-6 Carlson Orchards Apples, peeled
and sliced

1½ tsp cinnamon

3 tbsp butter

3 tbsp Green Friedman
All-Purpose Flour

½ cup Greenwood Farm Cider Syrup

⅓ cup Cook's Maple Syrup

1 tbsp lemon juice

- Cream shortening, sugar and salt.
- Add egg and 1 tbsp lemon juice; mix on low speed.
- Stir flour and baking powder together. Add to shortening mixture.
- Add milk, stirring until blended; set aside.
- Place apples in buttered 1½ qt baking dish.
- Stir cinnamon into the apples.
- Melt butter; mix with flour over low heat.
- Add cider syrup and maple syrup; stir until thickened.
- Blend in remaining 1 tbsp lemon juice; pour over apples.
- Spoon short dough over apples, spreading to completely cover.
- Bake at 400 degrees 25-30 minutes, or until golden brown.
- Serves 6.

New England Cranberry Sherbet

2 cups Ocean Spray Fresh Cranberries

2 cups sugar

3 tbsp lemon juice

2 cups Hood Milk

1 cup Hood Whipping Cream

- Wash and cook cranberries in water until tender.
- Press through potato ricer; add sugar and cook until sugar dissolves. Chill completely.
- Add lemon juice, milk and cream.
- Freeze in White Mountain Freezer according to manufacturer's directions.
- Makes 1½ qts.

Brie Pear Tart

1, 9" deep-dish pie shell
½ lb brie
3 eggs
¾ cup heavy cream
¼ cup Nashoba Valley Dry Pear Wine
¼ tsp ginger
¼ tsp cinnamon
1 tsp Cumworth Farm Honey
1 large Atkins Pear

- Bake pie shell at 350 degrees 5 minutes. Remove from pan.
- Reset oven to 375 degrees.
- Remove rind from brie. Chop rind into small pieces and reserve.
- Cream brie and eggs until smooth.
- Add cream, wine, ginger, cinnamon and honey. Mix until smooth.
- Sprinkle reserved rind in bottom of pie shell.
- Peel, core and thinly slice pear. Arrange slices over rind.
- Pour in liquid.
- Bake 45-60 minutes, until set and browned.
- Allow to cool 10 minutes before serving.
- Serves 6-8.

Green Tea Ice Cream

⅔ cup sugar
⅔ cup water
1 tsp vanilla
4-5 tsp Barrows Japanese Green Tea
2 cups Hood Half & Half

- In saucepan, over low heat, add sugar and water; heat until sugar dissolves.
- Simmer 3-4 minutes longer.
- Add vanilla; remove from heat.
- In small bowl, pulverize tea into dust. Add 2 tsp of dissolved sugar; stir well.
- Pour tea mixture into saucepan.
- Stir in cream; chill.
- Place chilled mixture into ice cream maker and churn until smooth and thick.
- Place in covered container; freeze at least 1 hour before serving.
- Serves 6-8.

Old-Fashioned Strawberry Ice Cream

1 cup milk

3 Ferruci Eggs, beaten

2 cups sugar, divided

⅛ tsp salt

1 tbsp all-purpose flour

2 cups Cooper's Hilltop Farm Heavy Cream, whipped

2 cups crushed Nourse Farms Strawberries

- Scald milk.
- Combine eggs, 1 cup sugar, salt and flour.
- Stir hot milk thoroughly and slowly into mixture.
- Heat in double boiler, stirring constantly, until mixture thickens. Remove from heat; cool.
- Fold in whipped cream.
- Freeze in White Mountain Freezer according to manufacturer's directions.
- Sprinkle remaining sugar on strawberries; stir into partially frozen mixture. Continue freezing.
- Makes 2 qts.

Blueberry Maple Mousse

6 egg yolks

⅔ cup Gould's Sugarhouse Maple Syrup, heated

1 pt West Lynn Creamery Heavy Cream

1 pt Tougas Farm Blueberries

- Beat yolks and place in top pan of double boiler until thick. Beat in hot syrup.
- Put over simmering water and cook, beating constantly until slightly thickened; cool.
- Beat cream until it forms stiff peaks; fold into yolk mixture.
- Fold in half of berries.
- Pour into 1½ qt mold. Freeze overnight.
- Before serving, garnish with remainder of berries.
- Serves 8-10.

Spiced Coffee Pudding

1 (2.25 oz) pkg Plymouth Rock Coffee
Gelatin Dessert

¼ cup light brown sugar

½ tsp ground cinnamon

pinch salt

1½ cups hot West Lynn Creamery Milk

½ cup West Lynn Creamery
Cream, whipped

3 gingersnap cookies, crumbled

- In medium bowl, combine coffee gelatin, brown sugar, cinnamon, salt and milk; stir until gelatin is dissolved.
- Chill until slightly thickened.
- Fold in whipped cream and pour into dessert dishes.
- Sprinkle tops with gingersnap crumbs; chill until firm.
- Serves 4-6.

Common Cracker Pudding
—100 Year Old Recipe

2 cups crushed Bent's
Common Crackers

6 cups All Star Dairy Milk

1 cup sugar

½ tsp cinnamon

1 tsp salt

1 tbsp butter

1 cup raisins

- Combine all ingredients, except raisins.
- Pour into buttered deep baking dish; bake 3 hours in 275 degree oven.
- Plump raisins over steam or hot water 10-15 minutes.
- After 30 minutes of baking, stir raisins into cracker mixture; continue baking.
- Drizzle additional milk around edges to prevent drying.
- Serves 10-12.

New England Indian Pudding

5 cups Garelick Farm Milk, divided
⅔ cup molasses
½ cup Gray's Yellow Corn Meal
⅓ cup sugar
1 tsp salt
¾ tsp Spice Up Your Life Cinnamon
¼ tsp Spice Up Your Life Nutmeg
¼ cup butter
heavy cream or vanilla ice cream

- Heat 4 cups of milk and molasses together.
- Combine corn meal, sugar, salt and spices; gradually stir into hot liquid. Add butter.
- Cook over low heat, stirring frequently until mixture thickens, about 20 minutes.
- Pour into greased 1½ qt baking dish. (A stone crock or electric bean pot can be used for baking).
- Pour remaining cool milk on pudding. Do not stir.
- Bake at 300 degrees 3 hours.
- Serve hot with heavy cream or vanilla ice cream.
- Serves 8-10.

Bread Pudding

3-4 cups diced dry Baldwin Hill Bread
3 cups Shaw's Dairy Milk
3 eggs
⅓ cup Ewen's Sleepy Hollow Sugarhouse Maple Syrup
1 tsp vanilla
½ tsp nutmeg
¼ cup chopped walnuts
¼ cup raisins
¼ cup Chicama Vineyards Raspberry Jam

- Soak bread in milk for 15 minutes.
- Combine eggs, maple syrup, vanilla and nutmeg; beat well.
- Add nuts, raisins and jam.
- Pour mixture over soaked bread; mix lightly with a fork until well blended.
- Bake pudding in baking dish or bread pan, set in pan of hot water, 45 minutes in 350 degree oven.
- Serve hot or cold.
- Serves 6-8.

Old-Fashioned Strawberry Shortcake

2 cups sifted all-purpose flour

¼ cup sugar

1 tbsp baking powder

½ tsp salt

½ cup butter

¾ cup Cooper's Hilltop Farm Milk

1 qt fresh Sunshine Farm Strawberries, sliced and sweetened

½ pt Cooper's Hilltop Farm Whipping Cream, whipped

- In bowl, sift together flour, sugar, baking powder and salt.
- Cut in butter until mixture resembles coarse meal.
- Add milk all at once; stir until dough clings together.
- On lightly floured surface, knead dough gently 10 times.
- Pat or roll dough ½" thick.
- Cut out 8 biscuits from dough with floured 2¾" diameter round cutter.
- Place on baking sheet, brush tops with milk.
- Bake at 450 degrees 10-15 minutes.
- To serve, split shortcakes, fill and top with strawberries.
- Serve with whipped cream.
- Serves 8.

CAKES

Pumpkin paradise, Amherst

Old Time Maple Gingerbread

2 cups all-purpose flour
1 tsp Hartman's Ground Ginger
1 tsp baking soda
½ tsp salt
1 cup Hill Tavern Farm Maple Syrup
1 egg, beaten
1 cup Czepiel's Sour Cream
maple hard sauce or whipped cream

- Combine and sift dry ingredients.
- Mix maple syrup with beaten egg; add sour cream.
- Combine mixtures; bake in moderate oven 40 minutes.
- Serve with warm maple hard sauce or whipped cream.
- Serves 8.

Maple Syrup Nut Cake

2¼ cups Green Friedman All-Purpose Flour
3 tsp baking powder
1 cup Orchard Farm Maple Syrup
½ cup Shady Oaks Farm Milk
1 cup chopped nuts
½ cup sugar
1 tsp salt
½ cup shortening
2 Johnson Poultry Farm Eggs

- Sift dry ingredients together into bowl.
- Add syrup, shortening and milk; beat 2 minutes.
- Add eggs and beat 2 minutes.
- Add chopped nuts and mix well.
- Pour into 2, greased and floured, 9" pans.
- Bake in 350 degree oven 25-30 minutes.
- Serves 18.

Apple Crumb Cake

1 cup butter

2 tbsp vegetable oil

¾ cup sugar

2 Parente Eggs

1 tsp vanilla

1 tsp lemon extract

1 tsp fresh lemon juice

2 cups all-purpose flour

2 tsp baking powder

3-4 Carlson Orchards Cortland Apples, thinly sliced

or

1 (8 oz) jar Carlson Orchards Apple Cider Jelly

Hood's Vanilla Ice Cream or Whipped Cream

Crumb Topping:

½ lb butter, melted, then cooled

2½ cups all-purpose flour

1 cup sugar

1 tsp almond extract

1 tsp vanilla

1 tsp lemon extract

- Preheat oven to 350 degrees.
- Cream together butter, oil and sugar.
- Add eggs, vanilla, lemon extract and lemon juice.
- Sift together flour and baking powder; add to butter mixture.
- Press into 9″ x 12″ greased pan.
- Add layer of apples or jelly (do not spread to edge of pan).
- Make crumb topping by mixing flour and sugar; combine with butter, vanilla and extracts.
- Mix crumb mixture with fingers until crumbly.
- Sprinkle over apples or jelly.
- Bake 25 minutes.
- Serve warm topped with ice cream or whipped cream.
- Serves 16-24.

Mrs. Cheney's Nobby Apple Cake

—New York & New England Apple Institute

¼ cup shortening
1 cup sugar
1 egg, beaten
½ tsp baking powder
½ tsp baking soda
½ tsp salt
½ tsp cinnamon
½ tsp nutmeg
1 cup all-purpose flour
3 cups cubed Massachusetts Apples
¼ cup chopped nuts (optional)
1 tsp vanilla
whipped cream or ice cream (optional)

- Cream shortening and sugar, add beaten egg.
- Sift dry ingredients.
- Add apples, nuts, vanilla and dry ingredients.
- Bake in greased 8″ square pan in 350 degree oven 45 minutes.
- Serve hot or cold, with whipped cream or ice cream, if desired.
- Serves 9.

Brick Oven Fruit Cake

—The Bake House, Old Sturbridge Village

1½ cups butter, softened
1 cup dark brown sugar
4 Johnson Poultry Farm Eggs, beaten
¼ cup molasses
1 lb seedless raisins
1 lb currants, plumped
½ lb citron, chopped
2 cups sifted Green Friedman All-Purpose Flour
1½ tsp Hartman's Cloves
1½ tsp Hartman's Cinnamon
1 tsp Hartman's Mace or Nutmeg
3 tbsp sherry
3 tbsp brandy

- Cream butter, mix in sugar until light and fluffy; add beaten eggs and molasses.
- Add raisins, plumped currants and citron.
- Sift flour with cloves, cinnamon and mace or nutmeg; stir into butter mixture.
- Mix thoroughly; stir in sherry and brandy.
- Prepare 9″ x 5″ loaf pan or 3 small loaf pans by greasing and lining with waxed paper or foil.
- Spread batter in pans.
- Bake at 300 degrees 1½ hours.
- Makes 1 large or 3 small fruit cakes.

Amid the hills, Lee

Jam Cake

1½ cups all-purpose flour

1 tsp baking soda

½ tsp salt

1 tsp allspice

¼ tsp cinnamon

¾ cup Czepiel's Buttermilk

2 tbsp West County Winery Orchards Edge Apple Raspberry Wine

⅓ cup shortening

½ cup sugar

½ cup firmly packed brown sugar

3 eggs, separated

½ cup The Herb Garden Raspberry Jam

2 squares unsweetened chocolate, melted and cooled

1 cup raisins

½ cup chopped nuts

powdered sugar

raspberries to garnish (optional)

- Mix flour, soda, salt and spices.
- In separate bowl, combine buttermilk and wine. Add shortening and cream.
- Gradually beat in sugars and continue beating until light and fluffy.
- Add egg yolks and beat thoroughly.
- Alternately add flour and buttermilk mixtures, beating after each addition until smooth.
- Blend in jam and chocolate. Fold in raisins and nuts.
- Beat egg whites until stiff peaks form; fold into batter.
- Pour into well-greased 9" tube pan. Bake at 350 degrees 50-55 minutes, or until toothpick inserted in center of cake comes out clean.
- Cool in pan 15 minutes.
- Remove sides of pan and finish cooling upright on rack.
- Loosen from tube and bottom; invert onto rack.
- Wrap in aluminum foil or plastic wrap. Store in refrigerator at least 2 days to mellow flavors.
- Serve at room temperature.
- Before serving, sprinkle with powdered sugar and garnish with raspberries, if desired.
- Serves 8-10.

Raspberry Pound Cake Delight

2¼ cups all-purpose flour

2 cups sugar

1 tsp grated lemon or orange peel

½ tsp salt

½ tsp baking soda

1 cup sour cream

1 cup butter, softened

1 tsp vanilla

3 eggs

Columbo Gourmet Raspberry Cheesecake Frozen Yogurt

fresh raspberries

- Preheat oven to 325 degrees.
- Generously grease and lightly flour 12 cup fluted tube pan.
- In large bowl, blend first 9 ingredients at low speed until moistened.
- Beat 3 minutes at medium speed. Pour batter into prepared pan.
- Bake 55-60 minutes, or until toothpick inserted in center comes out clean.
- To serve, place pound cake slices on individual dishes. Top with scoop of frozen yogurt and fresh raspberries.
- Serves 10-16.

Strawberry Cake Roll

3 Whip-O-Will Farm Eggs

1 tsp vanilla

1 cup sugar

⅓ cup water

1 tsp baking powder

½ tsp salt

1 cup all-purpose flour

powdered sugar

1 cup Cooper's Hilltop Farm Heavy Cream, whipped

4 cups sliced Nourse Farms Strawberries

- Preheat oven to 350 degrees.
- In large bowl, beat eggs with electric mixer until thick; add vanilla.
- Gradually beat in sugar, water, baking powder, salt and flour. Fold in egg mixture until smooth.
- Line 10" x 15" baking pan with waxed paper and grease; turn mixture into pan.
- Bake 12-15 minutes.
- Turn out onto tea towel lightly sprinkled with powdered sugar; peel off paper.
- Roll cake up in towel; cool. Unroll and spread with whipped cream and berries. Reroll.
- Refrigerate several hours for easier slicing.
- Serves 10.

Goat Cheesecake

2 cups crushed Sunbeam
Graham Crackers

¼ cup powdered sugar

6 tbsp melted butter

4 Johnson Poultry Farm Eggs,
separated

1⅓ cups sugar

⅓ cup Hood Whipping Cream or Milk

2 lbs Westfield Farm Capri
Goat Cheese

3 tbsp all-purpose flour

1 tsp vanilla

- For crust, mix first 3 ingredients, reserving small amount of cracker crumbs; shape into 10″ springform pan.
- Bake 10 minutes at 375 degrees; chill.
- Beat egg whites and egg yolks separately.
- Dissolve sugar in cream; add goat cheese, egg yolks, flour and vanilla. Fold in egg whites.
- Pour over crumb crust and bake 1 hour at 350 degrees.
- Serves 8-10.

Easy Cheesecake

1 cup sugar

1 lb Czepiel's Cream Cheese, softened

¼ cup The Herb Garden Raspberry
Wine Vinegar

3 eggs

1, 9″ graham cracker crust

fresh raspberries (optional)

- Cream sugar and cream cheese; add vinegar.
- Stir in 1 egg at a time until blended, scraping bowl after each addition.
- Place mixture in crust.
- Place cheesecake in large baking pan filled with ½″ water. Bake 1 hour at 325 degrees.
- Serve with fresh raspberries on top, if desired.

PIES

A tranquil Massachusetts harbor

Cheesecake Pie

1 cup Czepiel's Cream Cheese, softened

3½ cups whipped topping

⅓ cup sugar

2 tsp vanilla

2 cups Patt's Blueberries

graham crackers or
1, 9" unbaked pie shell

- Mix cream cheese, whipped topping, sugar and vanilla with electric mixer until smooth.
- Add blueberries.
- Spread mixture between 2 graham crackers, or fill pie shell.
- Serves 6-8.

Fresh Rhubarb Pie

⅓ cup Green Friedman All-Purpose Flour

2 cups sugar, or to taste

4 cups chopped Griggs Farm Rhubarb

pastry for 2 crust, 9" pie

1½ tbsp butter

sugar to garnish

- Mix flour with sugar; mix lightly with rhubarb.
- Pour into pie shell; dot with butter.
- Cover rhubarb mixture with top crust; cut slits in top crust.
- Sprinkle with sugar; seal and flute.
- Cover edge with 1½" strip of foil to prevent excessive browning.
- Bake in 425 degree oven 40-50 minutes, until juice begins to bubble through slits. Serve warm.
- Serves 8-10.

Crustless Pumpkin Pie

3 Ferruci Eggs

¾ cup Cumworth Farm Honey

1 tsp ginger

½ tsp nutmeg

½ tsp cinnamon

¼ tsp salt

1¾ cups Arena Farms Pumpkin

1 cup evaporated milk

- Slightly beat eggs; add honey, spices, salt and pumpkin.
- Mix well, add milk.
- Pour pumpkin custard into well greased, 9" glass pie pan.
- Bake at 325 degrees 1 hour, or until pie tests done. Cool thoroughly.
- Serve in wedges.
- Serves 8-10.

Fresh Pumpkin Pie

2 cups mashed cooked fresh Arena Farms Pumpkin

¾ cup firmly packed brown sugar

2 tsp cinnamon

¾ tsp salt

¾ tsp ginger

½ tsp nutmeg

⅛ tsp cloves (optional)

4 Sunny Rock Farm Eggs, slightly beaten

1½ cups Gibson Village Farm Dairy Light Cream or Milk

1, 9" unbaked pie shell

whipped cream

- Preheat oven to 400 degrees.
- Combine pumpkin and sugar.
- Blend in cinnamon, salt, ginger, nutmeg and cloves.
- Add eggs; gradually stir in cream or milk.
- Pour into pie shell.
- Bake 40-45 minutes, or until knife inserted near center comes out clean.
- Cool on wire rack. Top with whipped cream.
- Serves 8.

Massachusetts Apple Cranberry Pie

½ cup sugar

2 tbsp all-purpose flour

¼ tsp cinnamon

¼ tsp salt

1 tsp grated orange peel

½ cup Davenport Maple Farm Maple Syrup or Honey

1 tbsp butter

2 cups fresh Paradise Meadows Cranberries

3 cups sliced peeled Bluebird Acres McIntosh Apples

pastry for 2 crust, 9" pie

- Combine first 7 ingredients.
- Cook 2 minutes, stirring until sugar dissolves.
- Add cranberries; boil 2 minutes, or until cranberries burst.
- Fold in apple slices. Cool.
- Pour into pastry-lined 9" pie pan.
- Lattice strips of pastry over filling.
- Trim edges; flute.
- Bake at 425 degrees 35-40 minutes.

Vinegar Pie

1¼ cups sugar

¼ cup all-purpose flour

1 tbsp grated lemon peel

½ cup Chicama Vineyards
Raspberry Vinegar

2 cups water

3 Diemand Egg Farm Eggs, well beaten

1 tbsp butter

1, 9" unbaked pie shell

- Preheat oven to 425 degrees.
- Combine sugar, flour and lemon peel in saucepan.
- Add vinegar, stirring constantly, then add water.
- Bring to boil over medium heat and cook, stirring constantly, 1 minute.
- Remove from heat and stir a little of the hot mixture into eggs, then stir warmed eggs back into remaining hot mixture.
- Stir in butter.
- Pour mixture into pie shell and bake 10 minutes.
- Reduce heat to 350 degrees and bake 30 minutes more.
- Let cool completely before serving.
- Serves 8-10.

Frozen Peanut Butter Pie

3½ cups whipped topping, divided

1, 9" graham cracker crumb crust,
baked and cooled

⅓ cup Bear Meadow Farm Strawberry-
Rhubarb Jam

1 cup cold milk

½ cup chunky peanut butter

1 (3.5 oz) pkg vanilla instant pudding
and pie filling

chopped nuts to garnish

- Spread 1 cup whipped topping in bottom of pie crust; freeze 10 minutes.
- Carefully spoon jam over whipped topping.
- Gradually add milk to peanut butter in bowl, blending until smooth. Add pie filling mix.
- With electric mixer at low speed, beat until well blended, 1-2 minutes.
- Fold in remaining whipped topping. Spoon over jam in pie crust.
- Freeze until firm, about 4 hours.
- Garnish with additional whipped topping and chopped nuts, if desired.
- Serves 8-10.

Deep-Dish Apple Pie

—New York & New England Apple Institute

2½ qts (9-12) Massachusetts Apples,
pared and sliced
1½ cups sugar
½ tsp Hartman's Cinnamon
½ tsp Hartman's Nutmeg
¼ tsp salt
dash Hartman's Mace
3 tbsp butter
cream

Pastry:

1½ cups all-purpose flour
½ tsp salt
½ cup shortening
3 tbsp cold milk

- To make pastry, sift flour and salt. Cut in shortening with pastry blender until pieces are size of small pea.
- Add cold milk by teaspoonfuls, tossing with a fork until all flour-coated bits are barely dampened.
- Turn mixture onto a square of waxed paper.
- Gather up corners, pressing from the outside to form a compact ball.
- Roll out on floured board.
- Fill a 12″ x 8″ x 2″ oblong glass baking dish with apples.
- Mix dry ingredients and sprinkle over apples, mixing lightly. Dot with butter.
- Roll pie crust thin; place on top. Brush crust with cream, slit.
- Bake in 450 degree oven 15 minutes.
- Reduce heat to 350 degrees and cook 45 minutes longer.
- Serves 10-12.

Coffee Walnut Pie

1 (2.25 oz) pkg Plymouth Rock Coffee
Gelatin Dessert

1½ cups hot water

2 Parente Eggs, separated

pinch salt

2 tbsp maple extract

1, 8" graham cracker crumb crust

¾ cup coarsely chopped walnuts

whipped cream

- In medium bowl, combine coffee gelatin and water; stir until gelatin is dissolved.
- In small saucepan, beat egg yolks and salt together; gradually stir in gelatin.
- Heat slowly, stirring constantly, until mixture thickens and coats spoon.
- Chill until slightly thickened.
- In small bowl, beat egg whites until they form soft peaks.
- Fold into gelatin mixture with maple extract.
- Pour into crust and sprinkle top with nuts.
- Chill until firm.
- Serve with whipped cream.
- Serves 8.

Butternut Ice Cream Pie

2 cups mashed, cooked, fresh Wheeler
Farm Butternut Squash

¾ cup sugar

½ tsp salt

½ tsp ginger

½ tsp cinnamon

¼ tsp nutmeg

1 cup All Star Dairy Whipping
Cream, whipped

1 pt Friendly's Vanilla Ice Cream,
softened

1, 9" baked pie shell, chilled

whipped cream and chopped nuts
to garnish

- Combine fresh butternut squash, sugar, salt and spices; mix thoroughly.
- Fold in whipped cream.
- Spoon ice cream over bottom of pie shell, spread to edges.
- Spoon fresh butternut squash mixture on top; spread to edges. Freeze.
- Garnish with additional whipped cream and chopped nuts.
- Serves 8-10.

Peanut Butter Cup Frozen Yogurt Pie

1½ cup graham cracker crumbs

¼ cup sugar

⅓ cup melted butter or margarine

2 pts Colombo Gourmet Peanut Butter Cup Frozen Yogurt

½ cup fudge sauce

¼ cup chopped unsalted peanuts

whipped cream

- Heat oven to 375 degrees.
- In medium bowl, combine crumbs, sugar and melted butter; blend well.
- Press firmly into bottom and up the sides of 9" pie pan.
- Bake 8-10 minutes, or until golden brown.
- Cool completely.
- Soften frozen yogurt in refrigerator until just spreadable.
- Spread evenly into cooled crust.
- Freeze until firm, at least 2 hours.
- Just before serving, spread fudge sauce over frozen yogurt.
- Sprinkle peanuts on top of fudge sauce.
- Using a spoon or decorating tube, add whipped cream around outer edge of pie.
- Serve immediately.
- Serves 8-10.

Cider Pie

2 tbsp butter
2 tbsp all-purpose flour
½ cup Greenwood Farm Cider Syrup
½ cup Blue Heron Farm Maple Syrup
1 egg
5 Atkins Apples
pastry for 2 crust, 9″ pie

- Blend butter and flour.
- Gradually add syrups.
- Cook in double boiler until thick; cool.
- Add beaten egg.
- Peel, core and slice apples; place in pastry-lined 9″ pie pan and cover with the cider mixture.
- Cover with top crust and bake 50 minutes at 400 degrees.
- Serves 10-12.

Fudge Sundae Pie

¼ cup corn syrup
2 tbsp firmly packed brown sugar
3 tbsp butter
2½ cups Grainfield's® Crispy Rice Cereal
¼ cup peanut butter
¼ cup Chicama Vineyards Mocha Kahlua Sauce
3 tbsp corn syrup
1 qt Hendrie's Vanilla Ice Cream

- Combine corn syrup, brown sugar and butter in medium-size saucepan.
- Cook over low heat, stirring occasionally, until mixture begins to boil.
- Remove from heat.
- Add cereal, stirring until well coated.
- Press evenly in 9″ pie pan to form crust.
- Stir together peanut butter, fudge sauce and corn syrup.
- Spread half the peanut butter mixture over crust.
- Freeze until firm.
- Allow ice cream to soften slightly.
- Spoon into frozen pie crust, spreading evenly.
- Freeze until firm.
- Let pie stand at room temperature about 10 minutes before cutting.
- Warm remaining peanut butter mixture and drizzle over top.
- Serves 8.

COOKIES

A reflection of Autumn, Leverett

Purely Maple Drop Cookies

¾ cup butter, softened
¾ cup Graves' Sugarhouse Maple Syrup
1 large egg
1 tsp vanilla
3 cups New England Natural Bakers Maple Nut Granola
1 cup raisins
1⅓ cup Gray's Whole Wheat Flour
½ tsp baking soda

- Cream butter and maple syrup.
- Add egg and vanilla; mix well.
- Add remaining ingredients; mix well.
- Drop on greased cookie sheet by tablespoonfuls.
- Bake at 350 degrees for 10-12 minutes.
- Makes 2 doz.

Crisp and Cracklin' Rice Squares

2 cups New Morning Crispy Brown Rice Cereal
¾ cups Cumworth Farm Maple Syrup or Honey
2 tbsp melted butter
1 cup chopped cashews or peanuts

- Oil an 8″ x 8″ square pan.
- Stir together ingredients in bowl; place in pan, cover with waxed paper and press down with hand to spread evenly.
- Refrigerate 5 hours or more, or freeze 2 hours.
- Cut into bars and serve.
- Makes 1½ doz.

Peanut Butter Scotches

1 cup corn syrup

1 cup sugar

1 cup prepared Olde Tyme Peanut Butter

6 cups Grainfield's® Crispy Rice Cereal

1 (6 oz) pkg semi-sweet chocolate morsels

1 (6 oz) pkg butterscotch morsels

- In large saucepan, cook corn syrup and sugar over medium heat, stirring frequently, until mixture begins to boil.
- Remove from heat.
- Stir in peanut butter.
- Mix in cereal. Press in buttered 13" x 9" x 2" pan.
- Melt chocolate morsels and butterscotch morsels over hot (not boiling) water, stirring constantly until smooth.
- Spread over cereal mixture.
- Chill until firm, about 15 minutes; cut into bars.
- Makes 4 doz.

Honey Cranberry Cookies

1 cup shortening

½ cup brown sugar

2 Westminster Farm Eggs

1 cup honey

½ cup plain yogurt

1¾ cups all-purpose flour

1 tsp baking soda

1 tsp baking powder

¼ tsp salt

1 tsp nutmeg

1 tsp ginger

1 tsp cinnamon

3 cups quick-cooking rolled oats

1½ cups Ocean Spray Fresh Cranberries, chopped

½ cup chopped nuts

- Cream together shortening, sugar and eggs until fluffy.
- Stir in honey and yogurt.
- Sift together flour and next 6 ingredients; stir into creamed mixture.
- Stir in oats, berries and nuts; mix well.
- Drop by teaspoonfuls 2" apart on greased cookie sheets.
- Bake at 400 degrees 10 minutes.
- Makes 4 doz.

Oatmeal Raisin Cookies

1 cup La Spagnola Corn Oil

1 cup Cumworth Farm Maple Syrup or Honey

1 tsp vanilla

1 tsp baking soda

1 tsp cinnamon

¼ tsp nutmeg

3 cups New Morning Organic Quick Oats

1½ cups Gray's Whole Wheat Flour

1 cup raisins

- Preheat oven to 375 degrees.
- Mix together oil, maple syrup or honey and vanilla.
- Combine next 5 ingredients; add to oil mixture, mixing well.
- Stir in raisins and drop by rounded tablespoonfuls onto lightly oiled cookie sheet.
- Bake 8-9 minutes for a chewy cookie, 10-11 minutes for a crisp cookie.
- Makes 2 doz.

Graham Date

—The Bake-House, Old Sturbridge Village

1 cup dark brown sugar

½ cup sugar

¾ cup shortening

2 Westminster Farm Eggs

2 cups Green Friedman All-Purpose Flour

1 cup Green Friedman Whole Wheat Flour

1 tsp baking soda

2 tsp salt

2 tsp Hartman's Nutmeg

1 cup dates, finely chopped

2 tsp Charles H. Baldwin & Sons Vanilla

- Cream together sugars and shortening.
- Add eggs, 1 at a time, and beat well.
- Sift together flours, soda, salt and nutmeg; stir into batter and beat well.
- Fold in dates and vanilla.
- Beat several minutes until dates are thoroughly blended.
- Drop by teaspoonfuls onto cookie sheet.
- Bake at 375 degrees 12-15 minutes.
- Makes 2 doz.

BUYER'S GUIDE

Alcoholic Beverages

Boston Beer Company, Jamaica Plain
Chicama Vineyards (Chicama Vineyards), Martha's Vineyard
Inn Wines, Hatfield
Massachusetts Bay Brewing Company, Boston
Nantucket Vineyard, Nantucket
Nashoba Valley Winery (Nashoba Valley), Bolton
Plymouth Colony Winery, Plymouth
St. Vincent's Vineyard, Amherst
West County Winery (West County), Colrain
Via della Chiesa Vineyards, Raynham

Bakery

Au Bon Pain, Boston
Baldwin Hill Bakery (Baldwin Hill), Phillipston
Bart's Bakery, Northampton
Bent Company, G. H. (Bent's), Milton
Berger Limited, David, Medford
Berkshire Mountain Bakery, Housatonic
B J Foods, Inc., Hanson
Christina's Just Desserts, Housatonic
Concord Teacakes, Concord
Cook Sings, The, South Hamilton
Cookie Express, Dedham
Cookies to Scoop, Winchester
Freedman's Bakery (Freedman's Bakery), Brookline
"Let Them Eat Cake" Bakery, Lawrence
Montilios, Quincy
Near East Bakery, West Roxbury
Nejaime's of the Berkshires (Nejaime's Lavasch), Stockbridge
Riverside Restaurant & Bakery, Shelburne Falls
Roma Baking Company, Somerville
Sunbeam Bakery (Sunbeam), Dorchester
Venus/Old Brussels (Venus), Hingham
Wild About Chocolate, Acton

Beverages

Acadian Farms, Holliston
Allandale Farms, Brookline
Anderson Fruit Farm, Westford
Anthony Cider Mill, Adams
Apple Hill Farm, Dunstable
Arnold's Orchard, Westboro
Atkins Farms Fruit Marketing (Atkins, Atkins Fruit Bowl), Belchertown
Barrows Tea Company (Barrows), New Bedford
Bartlett's Orchard, Richmond
Baxter Echo Hill Orchards, Monson
Best Friends Cocoa, Newton
Big Apple, The, Wrentham
Bluebird Acres (Bluebird Acres), East Longmeadow
Bolton Orchards (Bolton Orchards), Bolton
Box Mill, Stow
Breezeland Orchards, Warren
Brewster's Store, Brewster
Brookfield Orchards, North Brookfield
Brooksby Farm, Peabody
Calzetto Farm, North Andover
Carlson Orchards, Inc. (Carlson Orchards), Harvard
Chase Farm Cider Mill, Inc., Littleton

Clarkdale Fruit Farm, West Deerfield
Community Supported Agriculture-Organic Apple Orchard, Egremont
Cook's Valley Farm (Cook's), Wrentham
Coutts & Son, Boxborough
Crow Farm, Sandwich
Davidian Farm, Northboro
Derby Orchards, Stow
Dowac Orchard, Sherborn
Drew Farms, Westford
Fay Mountain Fruit Farm, Charlton
Goodale Orchards, Ipswich
Green Acre Fruit Farm, Wilbraham
Hamilton Orchards, New Salem
Hartman's Herb Farm (Hartman's), Barre
Hillside Orchard, Granville
Hilltop Orchards, Richmond
Honey Pot Hill Orchards, Stow
Hubbardston Orchards, Hubbardston
Hutchins Farm, Concord
Johnnie's Cider Mill, South Easton
Lanni Brothers, Lunenberg
Lawson's Cider Mill, Lincoln
Lincoln Apple Juice (Lincoln), Brewster
Mann Orchards, Methuen
Marini Farm, Ipswich
Meadowbrook Orchards, Sterling
Millvale Farms & Cider Mill, Haverhill
Ocean Spray (Ocean Spray), Lakeville-Middleboro
Orchard Hill Farms, Haverhill
Outlook Farm, Westhampton
Pepsi-Cola South Headquarters (Pepsi-Cola), Dallas, TX
Peter's Cider Mill, Acushnet
Pine Hill Orchards, Colrain
Poyant Cider Mill, Acushnet
Price Cider Mill, Lunenberg
Razcal Corporation (Razcal), Sudbury
Red Apple Farm (Red Apple Farm), Phillipston
Rice Fruit Farm, Wilbraham
Rotondo's Farm Cider Mill, Concord
Scott Orchards, E & J, South Ashfield
Smith Cider Mill, Ira, West Bridgewater
Smith Farm, C. N., East Bridgewater
Taft Farm, Great Barrington
Touchstone Farm, Easthampton
View North Orchards, Three Rivers
Welch's (Welch's), Concord
Williamson's Cider Mill, Natick
Wyben Orchards, Westfield

Candy/Confectionary

Boomer's Cogies, Pittsfield
Cook's Biscotti, Brookline
Cookies Cook'n (Cookies Cook'n), Northboro
Diddies, Pittsfield
Goodjinipper's, Auburn
Green River Chocolates, Colrain
Harbor Sweets, Inc., Salem
Lawton Kitchens, Inc., Peggy, East Walpole
"Let Them Eat Cake" Bakery, Lawrence
Maleady's Madeleines, Hadley
Montilios, Quincy

Place Company (Rosa's Fudge), Springfield
Richardson's Candy Kitchen, Old Deerfield
Saccone's Toll House Bakery, Abington
Trombly's Peanut Butter Fantasies, Woburn
Truffle Mania, Worcester
VIP Sweets, Jamaica Plain

Cereals/Granolas

Energy Food Factory, Greenfield
New England Natural Bakers (New England Natural
  Bakers), Amherst
New Morning (New Morning), Acton
The Weetabix Company, Inc. (Alpen, Grainfield's),
  Clinton

Dairy/Cheese

Agri-Mark, Inc., Springfield
All Star Dairy Foods, Inc. (All Star Dairy), South
  Hadley
Bart's Ice Cream (Bart's), Greenfield
Bliss Brothers Dairy, Inc., Attleboro
Brigham's (Brigham's), Arlington
Brookside Farm (Brookside Farm), Fitchburg
Bryant Farm, Cummington
Carando (Carando), Springfield
Colombo, Inc. (Colombo), Andover
Cooper's Hilltop Farm (Cooper's Hilltop Farm),
  Rochdale
Craigston Cheese Company (Craigston), Wenham
Crescent Ridge Dairy, Inc. (Crescent Ridge Dairy),
  Sharon
Czepiel Dairy Foods, Inc. (Czepiel's), Ludlow
Dairy Center of Berkshires, Pittsfield
Dorchester Ice Cream Corporation, Dorchester
Dunajski Farm, Peabody
Edge Hill Farm, Cummington
Emack & Bolio's (Emack & Bolio's), Cambridge
Friendly Ice Cream Corporation (Friendly's), North
  Wilbraham
Garelick Farms (Garelick Farms), Franklin
Gibson Village Farm Dairy (Gibson Village Farm
  Dairy), Worcester
Hood, Inc., H. P. (Hood, Hendrie's), Boston
Howard Johnson's (Howard Johnson's), Quincy
Idlenot Dairy of Massachusetts, Inc., Hatfield
Lundreg & Jonaitis Dairy Farms, Inc., Shrewsbury
Madeiros Farm, Seekonk
Manny's Dairy Farm, Lancaster
Martin's Cheese Company, Westport
McCarthy Brothers Ice Cream Company, Whitman
Peaceful Meadows Dairy (Peaceful Meadows),
  Whitman
Pioneer Dairy, Inc., Southwick
Rawson Brook Farm (Monterey Chevr'e), Monterey
Richardson Farms, Middleton
Shady Oaks Farm (Shady Oaks Farm), Medway
Shaw's Dairy, Inc. (Shaw's Dairy), Dracut
Smith's Country Cheese (Smith's Country Cheese),
  Winchendon
Spring Hill Farm Dairy, Inc., Haverhill
Treadwell's Ice Cream, Danvers
West Lynn Creamery (West Lynn Creamery), Lynn
Windy Hamlet Farm, West Brookfield

Flour/Other Grain Mill Products

Gray Grist Mill (Gray's), Adamsonville, RI

Green Friedman Flour (Green Friedman), Boston
Hingham Grain & Spice Company, Hingham
Near East Food Products, Inc., Leominster
Northeastern Flour Company, Inc., Boston

Gift Baskets

Allandale Farms, Brookline
Apple Barn at Marshall Farm, Fitchburg
Atkins Farms Fruit Marketing (Atkins, Atkins Fruit
  Bowl), Belchertown
Bartlett's Orchard, Pittsfield
Bluebird Acres (Bluebird Acres), East Longmeadow
Bolton Orchards, Bolton
Brookfield Orchards, Inc., North Brookfield
Carlson Orchards, Inc. (Carlson Orchards),
  Harvard
Cheney Orchards, Brimfield
Chicama Vineyards (Chicama Vineyards), Martha's
  Vineyard
Cook's Maple Products (Cook's), Worthington
Cumworth Farm (Cumworth Farm), Cummington
Flat Hill Orchards, Lunenberg
Goodale Orchards, Ipswich
Idylwilde Farm (Idylwilde Farm), Acton
Keown Orchards, Wilkinsville
Long Hill Orchards, West Newbury
Nashoba Valley Winery, Inc. (Nashoba Valley),
  Bolton
New England Sampler, South Weymouth
Orchard Farm, Ashfield
Pine Hill Orchards, Colrain
Red Apple Farm (Red Apple Farm), Phillipston
Red Bucket Sugar Shack, Worthington
Smith's Country Cheese (Smith's Country Cheese),
  Winchendon
Taste of The Island, Vineyard Haven
Trappist Preserves, Spencer

Jams/Jellies/Preserves

Bear Meadow Farm (Bear Meadow Farm), Florida
Chicama Vineyards (Chicama Vineyards), Martha's
  Vineyard
Cumworth Farm (Cumworth Farm), Cummington
Herb Garden, The (The Herb Garden), Worthington
Jelly Shack of Cape Cod, Inc., East Falmouth
Trappist Preserves, Spencer

Meat

Blood Farm (Blood Farm), West Groton
Carando (Carando), Springfield
Ottman Custom Processors, Inc. (Ottman), Sutton
Outlook Farm (Outlook Farm), Westhampton

Miscellaneous

Abruzzi Foods, Inc., Newton
Adit Corporation (Plymouth Rock Gelatin
  Desserts), Wayland
Bayajian, Cambridge
Berkshire Pasta Company, Pittsfield
Eleanor & Company, South Egremont
Harbar Corporation Tortillas, Jamaica Plain
Hot Mama's Super Natural Foods, Millers Falls
Kettle Cuisine, Revere
Nasoya, Leominster
Ocean Spray (Ocean Spray), Lakeview-Middleboro

Trio's Original Italian Products Company, Inc. (Trio's), Chelsea

Oils/Nuts/Seeds

Catania-Spagna, Inc. (La Spagnola), Somerville
New England Natural Bakers (New England Natural Bakers), Amherst

Poultry/Eggs

Asack Turkey Farm, West Bridgewater
B & E Turkey Roost, Jefferson
Belwing Acres Turkey Farm, Seekonk
Bennett's Turkey Farm, Wilbraham
Bob's Turkey Farm, Lancaster
Bongi's Turkey Roost, Duxbury
Boundary Farm, Essex
Burgner Farm Products, Pittsfield
Diemand Egg Farm (Diemand Egg Farm), Millers Falls
Ferruci Egg Farm (Ferruci), Milford
Green Acres Turkey Farm, Wrentham
Hillside Poultry Farm (Hillside Farm), Truro
Johnson & Sons Poultry Farm (Johnson Poultry Farm), Westminster
Many Hands Organic Farm, Barre
Mar-Fran's Turkey Ranch, Granby
Mello Lane Turkey Farm (Mello Lane), Marlboro
Otis Poultry (Otis), Otis
Out Post Farm (Out Post Farm), Holliston
Owens Poultry Farm, Needham Heights
Parente's Poultry Farm (Parente), Mansfield
Pine Hill Farm (Pine Hill Farm), Southampton
Raymond's Turkey Farm, Methuen
Seven Acres Farm, North Reading
Sunny Acres Turkey Farm, East Longmeadow
Sunny Rock Farm (Sunny Rock Farm), Walpole
Twin Willows Turkey Farm (Twin Willows), Belchertown
Westminster Farm (Westminster Farm), Westminster
Whip-O-Will Farm (Whip-O-Will Farm), Southbridge

Fresh Produce

Allandale Farm, Brookline
Andrews Farm (Andrews Farm), East Falmouth
Arena Farms (Arena Farms), Concord
Atkins Farms Fruit Marketing, Inc. (Atkins, Atkins Fruit Bowl), Belchertown
Baxter's Echo Hill Orchard, Monson
Bay State Produce Company, Inc., Chelsea
Bean Farm, Westwood
Berberian Farms (Berberian Farms), Northboro
Bluebird Acres (Bluebird Acres), East Longmeadow
Bolton Orchards (Bolton Orchards), Bolton
Bolton Spring Farm (Bolton Spring Farm), Bolton
Carlson Orchards, Inc. (Carlson Orchards), Harvard
Cerasuolo, Inc., John, Chelsea
Cheney Orchards, Brimfield
Clegg Farms (Clegg Farms), Seekonk
Costa Fruit & Produce, Boston
D. Arrigo Brothers of Massachusetts, Chelsea
Dargoonian Farm (Dargoonian Farm), Andover
Decas Brothers Fruit & Produce, Inc. (Paradise Meadows), Wareham

Delftree Corporation (Delftree), North Adams
Demarco Produce Company, Inc., Malden
Dowse Orchards, Sherborn
Eastern Potatoes by Mish Potato Packers (Tater Delight), Hadley
Flavorful Sprouts, Greenfield
Fowler Farm (Fowler Farm), Westfield
Gove Farm (Gove Farm), Leominster
Griggs Farm (Griggs Farm), Billerica
Hamilton Orchards, New Salem
Hibbard Farm (Hibbard Farm), Hadley
Hutchins Farm, Concord
Idylwilde Farm (Idylwilde Farm), Acton
Ingalsby Farm, West Boxford
Jonathan's Agricultural Enterprises, Inc. (Jonathan's), Marion
Sullivan & Company, Joseph P., Ayer
MacArthur Farms, Holliston
Marini Farm (Marini Farm), Ipswich
Mohawk Orchards, Shelburne Falls
Nashoba Valley Winery (Nashoba Valley), Bolton
New England Truffle Company, Pittsfield
Nourse Farms, Inc. (Nourse Farms), South Deerfield
Noyes & Bimber, Inc., Chelsea
Ocean Spray (Ocean Spray), Lakeview-Middleboro
Outlook Farm (Outlook Farm), South Natick
Patt's Blueberries (Patt's), Holliston
Red Apple Farm (Red Apple Farm), Phillipston
Spence Farm (Spence Farm), Woburn and Reading
Sunshine Farm (Sunshine Farm), Framingham
Tougas Farm (Tougas Farm), Northboro
Verrill Farm (Verrill Farm), Concord
Volante Farm (Volante Farm), Needham
Wheeler Farm, North Reading
Wilson Farm (Wilson Farm), Lexington

Salad Dressings/Condiments

Adams Corporation, Henry C., Mattapoisett
Bear Meadow Farm (Bear Meadow Farm), Florida
Cain Company, John E. (Cains), Ayer
Chicama Vineyards (Chicama Vineyards), Martha's Vineyard
Dixie & Nikita, Inc. (Dixie & Nikita), Boston
Herb Garden, The (The Herb Garden), Worthington
India Classics, Inc., Reading
Marilyn's Sauces, Inc., Newburyport
Oxford Pickle Company, South Deerfield
Sloan Tavern Company (Sloan Tavern), Williamstown
Wolf Hill Farm, Southboro

Seafood

AquaFuture, Montague
Aslanis Seafoods (Pier 12), Boston
Bay State Lobster Company, Inc., Boston
Bioshelters, Inc., Amherst
Captain Mardens Sea Foods, Inc., Wellesley
Foley Company, M. F., Boxton
Hook & Company, James, Boston
Ipswich Shellfish Company, Inc., Ipswich
O'Hara & Sons, Inc., F. J., Boston
Orleans Clambake Company, Orleans
Red Wing Meadow Farm, Sunderland

Slade Gorton & Company, Inc. (Tem-Tasty,
    Gorton's, Icybay, SeaTasty, Campeche Marisol),
    Boston
Stavis Seafoods, Inc., Boston

Snacks

Goodwives, Marblehead
Hommus Factory, The, Sudbury
Jonathan's Agricultural Enterprises, Inc.
    (Jonathan's), Marion
New England Natural Bakers (New England Natural
    Bakers), Amherst
Shoanna's Gourmet Goodies, Inc., North Easton
State Line Snacks Corporation (State Line),
    Wilbraham
The Hommus Factory, Sudbury
Tri-Sum Potato Chip Company, Inc. (Tri-Sum,
    Suncrisp), Leominster
Vincent Potato Chip Company, Inc., Salem

Spices/Herbs

Berkshire Gardens, Southbridge
Creative Seasonings, Salem
East India Spice, Inc. (East India), Cambridge
General Spice, Inc., Malden
Greener Gardens, Holliston
Hartman's Herb Farm (Hartman's), Barre
Harvest Farms, Whatley
Hingham Grain & Spice Company, Hingham
Little Fox Spice Company, Inc., The, Wilborn
Mrs. G's Herbs, Inc. (Mrs. G's), Westford
Spice Up Your Life, Waltham
Wolf Hill Farm, Southboro

Sugar/Honey/Syrup

Amstar Corporation, Charlestown
Ares, Paul E., Sharon
Bee Happy Farm, Marston Mills
Beekeepers Warehouse, Woburn
Blue Heron Farm, Charlemont
Broff's Honey Products, Middleton
Brookside Farm, Westminster
Cook's Maple Products (Cook's), Worthington
Cumworth Farm (Cumworth Farm), Cummington
Davenport Maple Farm (Davenport), Shelburne
    Falls
Ewen's Sleepy Hollow Sugarhouse & Cider Mill
    (Ewen's), Lunenburg
Fern Hill Farm, Pembroke
Gould's Sugarhouse, Shelburne
Graves' Sugarhouse, Shelburne
Greenwood Farm (Greenwood Farm), Northfield
Harris, Jonathan, Avon
Hayden, David, West Bridgewater
Heemskerk, John, Needham
Hill Tavern Farm, South Egremont
K. E. Farm, Sturbridge
Lees' Bees, Lexington
Magee, Jr., Frederick L., West Bridgewater
Mt. Toby Sugarhouse, Sunderland
New Morning (New Morning), Acton
Orchard Farm (Orchard Farm), Ashfield
Orosz, Charlie, Plymouth
Phillips, John, Hanson
Podunk Pollinators, East Brookfield
Red Bucket Sugar Shack, Worthington
Wolf Hill Farm, Southboro

INDEX

Appetizers & Snacks

Baked Baby Gouda 23
Blue Goat Cheese
   Hors d'Oeuvres. 23
Cheddar Fondue 24
Cheese Puffs. 24
Chicken Almond Spread 22
Chips and Shrimp 21
Green Chili Hors d'Oeuvres . . . 22
Oatiola 25
Parmesan Garlic Artichokes. . . 24
Peppered Ham and
   Cream Cheese 23
Pepperoni Pate 25
Sesame Hoomus. 22
Shrimp Dip 20
Spicy Dip 20
Stuffed Quahogs. 21
Turkey Swedish Meatballs. 26
Wicked Awesome Bull Dip. 20

Beverages

Apple Strawberry Refresher . . 29
Cranberry Holiday Punch 29
Grand Grape Granite 29
Great Grape Iced Tea. 28
Hot Cranberry Cider 30
Peach Tea 28
Sparkling Tea Punch 30
Spiked Hare Punch. 30
Tea Cooler. 28

Breads

Banana Bread 53
Blueberry Coffeecake 56
Cheese Muffinettes. 58
Cranberry Coffee Braid. 55
Cranberry Fruit Nut Bread. . . . 54
Granola Carrot Bread 53
Jordan Marsh
   Blueberry Muffins. 58
Milk and Honey Bread 54
Oat Bran Muffins 57
Oyster Stuffing for Turkey 57
Pam's Zucchini Bread. 52

Pumpkin Bread 52
Raisin Bran Muffins. 55

Soups

Clam Chowder 80
Corn Chowder. 76
Fish Chowder 80
Fresh Tomato Soup. 79
Hearty Bean Soup 82
Iced Spinach Soup 79
Minted Summer Squash Soup. . 78
Pesto Tortellini Soup 77
Polish Potato Soup 80
Salmon and Scallop Stew with
   Hard Cider and Ginger. 82
Shiitake Mushroom Bisque 81
Spanish Gazpacho 78
Spinach Soup. 76
Zucchini and Cheddar
   Cheese Soup 77

Salads

Apple and Tarragon Salad
   with Watercress 86
Autumn Pear 'N Apple Salad. . . 85
Carrot Plus Three Salad 87
Cider Cole Slaw 86
Cranberry Wreath Salad 84
French Quarter Rice Salad 89
German Potato Salad and
   Sour Cream. 89
Italian Pasta Salad 91
Pesto Tortellini Salad. 91
Sliced Beet and Cucumber
   Salad with Creamy
   Herb Dressing. 87
Tabouli and Sprouts Salad 88
Tangy Cole Slaw 88
Tomato Vinaigrette 85
Unique Veronique Salad 84

Sauces

Blueberry Sauce. 100
Camembert Sauce 102
Dazzling Dessert Sauce. 100
Hot Coffee Ice Cream Sauce . . 100

Marinade for Fish
   or Chicken.............. 102
Quick and Easy
   Salad Dressing 101
Raspberry Poppy
   Seed Dressing........... 101
Simple Barbecue Sauce...... 102
Tangy Barbecue Sauce....... 102
Tasty Mustard
   Salad Dressing 101

Main Dishes

Barbara's Tomato Quiche 104
Betsy's Sprout Salad
   Pockets 106
Butternut-Sausage Quiche ... 105
Camembert French
   Bread Pizza.............. 106
Chicken Cacciatore 107
Easy Elegant Brunch........ 104
Hard Cider Casserole........ 105
Indian Pan-Fried Fish 109
Malabar Seafood Curry...... 109
Meat Stuffed Zucchini....... 107
Microwave Lamb Curry 108
Skillet Scallops............. 110
Super Sprout Pockets 110
Zesty Joes 108

Meats & Fish

Beef

Apple and Veal Scallop....... 124
Apple Meatloaf 126
Cranberry Pot Roast 126
Medallions of Veal with Tomatoes
   and Shiitake Mushrooms... 124
Prosciutto Veal Rolls Italiano 127
Swiss Veal Delight 125

Chicken

Chicken Breasts in Mushroom
   Wine Sauce 129
Chicken with Red Grapes 130
Lemon Chicken............. 130
Mustard Chicken 128
Wicked Awesome
   Dixie Chicken............ 128

Pork

Barbecued Pork Chops 127
Left-Over Holiday Ham...... 128

Seafood

Cod Fish Florentine 132
Honey's Baked Fish Filets.... 131
Lobster Newburg........... 131
Smelts with Beer Batter 132

Pasta

Chicken Breast Filets and
   Mushroom Sauce 142
Fettuccine Scampi
   and Broccoli 144
Fettuccine Alfredo.......... 143
Lemon Turkey Primavera 145
Pasta with Shiitake Mushrooms
   and Asparagus............ 141
Scallops with Broccoli
   and Noodles.............. 140
Spinach-Prosciutto Rolls..... 143
Turkey Lasagne 144
Turkey Tetrazzini........... 142

Vegetables

Baked Stuffed Squash 166
Broccoli with Sour Cream
   and Cashews............. 164
Broiled Tomatoes with Dill
   Sour Cream Sauce 161
Cauliflower and Mushrooms
   with Cheese Sauce........ 160
Corn Oysters 163
Dilled Baby Carrots......... 168
Fresh Creamed Corn 162
Grilled Tomatoes 162
Leeks and Cider 167
Mushroom Tempura........ 167
Potatoes Romano 168
Ratatouille 164
Sauteed Shiitake
   Mushrooms.............. 163
Spinach Roma.............. 161
Squash Apple Casserole 166
Stuffed Potatoes............ 168
Zucchini Provencale 165
Zucchini Stir-Fry 165

Desserts

Apple Cobbler with
  Cider Syrup.............. 184
Blueberry Maple Mousse 187
Bread Pudding 189
Brie Pear Tart.............. 185
Common Cracker Pudding ... 188
Green Tea Ice Cream........ 185
New England Cranberry
  Sherbet 184
New England Indian
  Pudding................. 189
Old-Fashioned Strawberry
  Ice Cream 187
Old-Fashioned Strawberry
  Shortcake 190
Spiced Coffee Pudding....... 188

Cakes

Apple Crumb Cake 193
Brick Oven Fruit Cake 195
Easy Cheesecake 198
Goat Cheesecake 198
Jam Cake 196
Maple Syrup Nut Cake....... 192
Mrs. Cheney's Nobby
  Apple Cake 195
Old Time Maple
  Gingerbread 192
Raspberry Pound
  Cake Delight............. 197
Strawberry Cake Roll 197

Pies

Butternut Ice Cream Pie 204
Cheesecake Pie 200
Cider Pie 206
Coffee Walnut Pie........... 204
Crustless Pumpkin Pie 200
Deep-Dish Apple Pie 203
Fresh Rhubarb Pie 200
Fresh Pumpkin Pie.......... 201
Frozen Peanut Butter Pie 202
Fudge Sundae Pie........... 206
Massachusetts Apple
  Cranberry Pie............ 201

Peanut Butter Cup Frozen
  Yogurt Pie 205
Vinegar Pie 202

Cookies

Crisp and Cracklin'
  Rice Squares............. 208
Graham Date................ 210
Honey Cranberry Cookies ... 209
Oatmeal Raisin Cookies 210
Peanut Butter Scotches...... 209
Purely Maple Drop Cookies .. 208

EQUIVALENTS

3 tsp.	1 tbsp.
4 tbsp.	1/4 cup
5 1/3 tbsp.	1/3 cup
8 tbsp.	1/2 cup
10 2/3 tbsp.	2/3 cup
12 tbsp.	3/4 cup
16 tbsp.	1 cup
1/2 cup	1 gill
2 cups	1 pint
4 cups	1 quart
4 quarts	1 gallon
8 quarts	1 peck
4 pecks	1 bushel
16 oz.	1 pound
1 oz. liquid	2 tbsp.
8 oz. liquid	1 cup
32 oz. liquid	1 quart

(For liquid and dry measurements use standard measuring spoons and cups. All measurements are level.)

WEIGHTS AND MEASURES

Baking powder
1 cup = 5 1/2 oz.

Corn meal
1 lb. = 3 cups

Cornstarch
1 lb. = 3 cups

Cracker crumbs
23 soda crackers = 1 cup
15 graham crackers = 1 cup

Eggs
1 egg = 4 tbsp. liquid
4 to 5 whole = 1 cup
7 to 9 whites = 1 cup
12 to 14 yolks = 1 cup

Flour
1 lb. all-purpose = 4 cups
1 lb. cake = 4 1/2 cups
1 lb. graham = 3 1/2 cups

Shortening or Butter
1 lb. = 2 cups

Sugar
1 lb. brown = 2 1/2 cups
1 lb. cube = 96 to 160 cubes
1 lb. granulated = 2 cups
1 lb. powdered = 3 1/2 cups

POTATO CHIPS

SUNCRISP® 7 oz. or larger
100% Sunflower Oil

Salted or No Salt Added

30¢ NO DOUBLE COUPONING

MR. GROCER: We will reimburse you for the face amount of the coupon plus 8¢ per coupon for handling provided you and consumer have complied with the terms of this offer. Invoices proving purchase of sufficient stock of our brand(s) to cover coupons presented for redemption must be shown upon request. Consumer must pay any sales tax. Coupon may not be transferred or assigned and is void where its use is prohibited, taxed or otherwise restricted. Cash value 1/20¢. This offer is limited to one coupon per purchase. Redeem by mailing to **Tri-Sum Potato Chip Co., Inc., 68 Cedar St., Leominster, Mass. 01453**

One Coupon Per Purchase

30¢

TORTILLA CHIPS

SUNCRISP® 10 oz. or larger
100% SAFFLOWER OIL

"BLUE" CORN CHIPS
"NATURAL" CORN CHIPS

30¢ NO DOUBLE COUPONING

MR. GROCER We will reimburse you for the face amount of the coupon plus 8¢ per coupon for handling provided you and consumer have complied with the terms of this offer. Invoices proving purchase of sufficient stock of our brand(s) to cover coupons presented for redemption must be shown upon request. Consumer must pay any sales tax. Coupon may not be transferred or assigned and is void where its use is prohibited, taxed or otherwise restricted. Cash value 1/20¢. This offer is limited to one coupon per purchase. Redeem by mailing to **Tri-Sum Potato Chip Co., Inc., 68 Cedar St., Leominster, Mass. 01453**

One Coupon Per Purchase

30¢

PREMIUM POPCORN

SUNCRISP® 6 oz. (168g)
100% Sunflower Oil

No Cholesterol — No Preservatives

40¢ NO DOUBLE COUPONING

MR. GROCER: We will reimburse you for the face amount of the coupon plus 8¢ per coupon for handling provided you and consumer have complied with the terms of this offer. Invoices proving purchase of sufficient stock of our brand(s) to cover coupons presented for redemption must be shown upon request. Consumer must pay any sales tax. Coupon may not be transferred or assigned and is void where its use is prohibited, taxed or otherwise restricted. Cash value 1/20¢. This offer is limited to one coupon per purchase. Redeem by mailing to **Tri-Sum Potato Chip Co., Inc., 68 Cedar St., Leominster, Mass. 01453**

One Coupon Per Purchase

40¢

MANUFACTURER'S COUPON | EXPIRES 5/15/91

40¢ Off

HERE'S 40¢ TO TRY NEW COLOMBO GOURMET FROZEN YOGURT.
(GOOD ON PINTS ONLY)

TO GROCER: You are authorized to act as our agent for the redemption of this coupon. We will reimburse you 40¢ on any purchase of Colombo Gourmet Frozen Yogurt plus 8¢ for handling if it has been used in accordance with our customer offer. Invoice proving purchase of sufficient stock to cover coupon presented for redemption must be shown on request. Coupon is void if taxed, prohibited or otherwise restricted by law. Customer pays any sales tax. Cash value 1/20 cent. Mail Coupon to: Colombo, Inc., P.O. Box 730400, El Paso, TX 79973.

Heath® is a registered trademark of Leaf, Inc.

Redeem at your local supermarket. 500089

MANUFACTURER'S COUPON

30¢

Save 30¢ on a quart of Cains® Mayonnaise
(Regular, Light, Or Cholesterol Free.)

Mr. Grocer. You may act as our agent for the redemption of this coupon. We will reimburse you 30¢ plus 8¢ handling if it has been used in accordance with our offer. Invoice proving purchase of sufficient stock to cover coupons presented for redemption must be shown on request. Coupons void if taxed, prohibited, or restricted by law. Customer pays any sales tax. Cash value is 1/20¢. Mail coupons to: John E. Cain Co., 114 East Main Street, Ayer, MA 01432.

30¢

10¢

Venus®

9022

Manufacturer's Coupon

ATTENTION CONSUMERS: Only use this coupon to purchase the specified product. You must pay any sales tax. ATTENTION RETAILERS: Venus Wafers Inc. CMS – Dept. 41651 One Fawcett Drive Del Rio, TX 78840 will reimburse you the face value of the coupon plus 8¢ provided you sold the named product at the retail level and on request furnish proof of purchase of sufficient product to cover all redemptions. Coupon not legitimately redeemed could violate FEDERAL U.S. MAIL STATUTES. Void when duplicated transferred, assigned taxed, restricted, or where prohibited. Any coupons submitted deemed fraudulent will be held. Cash value 1/100 cent. LIMIT ONE COUPON PER PURCHASE.

Venus Wafers Inc.

10¢

10¢

4 1651 00017

MASSACHUSETTS
Recipes for all Seasons
Additional $2 savings

- A $19.95 value offered at a special discount of $14.95
- Massachusetts coupons inside the book are valued over $20

Please send ___ copy (copies) of **MASSACHUSETTS Recipes for all Seasons** @ $14.95/copy, plus $2.50 freight to: (Make check or money order out to Leisure Time Publishing, 9029 Directors Row, Dallas, TX. 75247)

Name: _____

Address: _____

City/State/Zip:_____ Phone:_____

MASSACHUSETTS
Recipes for all Seasons
Additional $2 savings

- A $19.95 value offered at a special discount of $14.95
- Massachusetts coupons inside the book are valued over $20

Please send ___ copy (copies) of **MASSACHUSETTS Recipes for all Seasons** @ $14.95/copy, plus $2.50 freight to: (Make check or money order out to Leisure Time Publishing, 9029 Directors Row, Dallas, TX. 75247)

Name: _____

Address: _____

City/State/Zip:_____ Phone:_____

MASSACHUSETTS
Recipes for all Seasons
Additional $2 savings

- A $19.95 value offered at a special discount of $14.95
- Massachusetts coupons inside the book are valued over $20

Please send ___ copy (copies) of **MASSACHUSETTS Recipes for all Seasons** @ $14.95/copy, plus $2.50 freight to: (Make check or money order out to Leisure Time Publishing, 9029 Directors Row, Dallas, TX. 75247)

Name: _____

Address: _____

City/State/Zip:_____ Phone:_____